CASES IN

ADVERTISING
MANAGEMENT

Case Analysis Manual

Terence Nevett

NTC Business Books
NTC a division of *NTC Publishing Group* • Lincolnwood, Illinois USA

Published by NTC Business Books, a division of NTC Publishing Group.
© 1992 by NTC Publishing Group, 4255 West Touhy Avenue,
Lincolnwood (Chicago), Illinois 60646-1975 U.S.A.

2 3 4 5 6 7 8 9 ML 9 8 7 6 5 4 3 2 1

Contents

Guide to the Topics Covered in the Cases

Topics Covered

TELEPHONE, USE OF	TARGET AUDIENCE, SELECTION OF	SMALL BUDGET CAMPAIGNS	SERVICE ORGANIZATIONS, ADVERTISING FOR	SENIOR MANAGEMENT, RELATIONS WITH	RETAIL ADVERTISING	RESEARCH	PSAs	PROMOTIONS	PROFESSIONAL SERVICES, ADVERTISING OF	NOT-FOR-PROFIT ORGANIZATIONS	MEDIA SELECTION/PLANNING	INTERNATIONAL ADVERTISING	GENDER ROLE, STEREOTYPING	FREE SPEECH	ETHICAL CONSIDERATIONS IN ADVERTISING	DIRECT MARKETING/MAIL ORDER	DAMAGE CONTROL	CREATIVE STRATEGY/POSITIONING	COUNTRY-OF-ORIGIN/CROSS-CULTURAL FACTORS	COOPERATIVE CAMPAIGNS	CONSUMER COMPLAINTS	CHILDREN, ADVERTISING TO	CELEBRITY ENDORSEMENTS	BUSINESS-TO-BUSINESS ADVERTISING	AGENCY MANAGEMENT	AGENCY-CLIENT RELATIONS	ADVERTISING BUDGET	Case Title
		×								×	×																	THE BLOOMINGTON DISTRICT
×		×							×								×		×									FANSTONE'S FUNERAL HOMES
		×			×																							ANGELA'S FLOWERS ON FOURTH
											×	×						×										B.I. CYCLES OF MADRAS, INDIA
																									×			ENGLANDER ADVERTISING AGENCY
											×							×										REVLON COSMETICS ADVERTISING
												×					×			×								MEDS TAMPONS IN AUSTRALIA
								×			×							×										HUGGIES PULL-UPS®
		×						×			×							×										HARRY H. GUBBARD, D.D.S.
											×	×			×			×										TRAFFIC SIGN VANDALISM IN IOWA
		×									×							×										RIVERSEDGE MARKETING, INC.
	×																×	×					×					ASPEN SKIING COMPANY ADS
														×														CANYON BREWERIES: GLOSTER BEER
						×												×				×						JACOBS LABORATORIES TASK FORCE
		×			×													×										SHARPVISION OPTICAL COMPANY
						×																					×	RACHMAN'S DISCOUNT STORE
	×	×																×										CARSWELL'S RESTAURANT CHAIN
	×				×									×				×										SUNBURST ORANGE JUICE, FLORIDA
																									×	×		KARLIN-MARTIN ADVERTISING
					×								×					×	×									ALMA CHEESE CO., AUSTRIA
	×	×		×	×													×										MAGELLAN LUXURY TRAVEL
	×											×		×	×			×				×						LITTLE TYKES TOY COMPANY
	×				×				×									×										MICHIGAN LOTTERY—KENO
			×			×										×	×											PEER BROTHERS VACATIONS
												×						×										N.Z. KIWIFRUIT AUTHORITY (B)
				×									×	×	×													UNITED CHEMICAL PRODUCTS
	×	×			×			×		×								×										TREES ATLANTA'S CROSSROADS
	×	×		×				×			×							×										MARFIO'S TIJUANA TAKEOUT
	×										×					×		×										NEAT 'N TIDY: FINE ACCESSORIES
	×	×	×								×							×		×								PORTAGE LAKE CHARTER FISHING
												×	×					×									×	KLEIDER INTERNATIONAL CLOTHING
					×						×							×										TEXAS TAPES AUDIO STORES
	×											×	×					×	×		×							A&A ELECTRIC LIMITED OF INDIA
				×				×							×			×										WALPURGIS FILMS—HOME VIDEOS

Introduction

USING THE CASES

Cases in Advertising Management is intended for use by students in both Business and Journalism Schools and can be used either as the basis for a case study class or to supplement a course text. It also aims to provide the instructor with a high degree of flexibility in adapting it to the needs of a particular class. Variations in the length, complexity and subject matter of the cases allow the instructor to select those most suited to his/her students. Questions on the cases are included in this manual rather than in the book itself, which allows the instructor to control the amount of guidance available to students. The cases may also be employed in a variety of learning situations.

This collection of cases is intended to benefit students in a number of ways. The underlying emphasis is on conveying the realities of the workplace and providing an understanding of what managing an organization's advertising actually involves, rather than confronting students with a sophisticated form of academic exercise. By providing a sample of the kinds of decisions likely to be faced in advertising management, the book gives students vicarious or simulated experience, and allows them to make some of the more basic mistakes before they have reached a situation where it can affect their careers. As an anonymous wit once remarked, lawyers have their mistakes locked away behind bars, doctors have theirs buried six feet under ground, and advertisers put theirs on television during prime time.

Because cases in the book are not grouped by category, students have to define what kind of problem they are dealing with and set the limits within which a suitable course of action must be decided. This reflects the fact that real life problems come in a wide range of shapes and sizes, and need to be examined carefully to determine that they are in fact what they appear to be. A problem that arrives on an advertising manager's desk may have been designated an advertising problem by someone else in the organization (falling sales would be an obvious example), but closer examination may reveal that the cause lies elsewhere.

The diversity of the cases should also help students appreciate the wide range of organizational settings in which advertising decisions routinely have to be made. Cases cover the manufacturing, service, and not-for-profit sectors, with variations in organizational size from the multinational corporation to the one-person business. This diversity should also help students understand how the advertising function, and the constraints under which advertising managers have to work, can vary from one type of organization to another. The manager in a large manufacturing company may have a big budget but little authority, whereas in a small company advertising might be handled directly by the owner, so the reverse would hold true. Also, while the manager in a large organization may be able to research and plan in something resembling textbook fashion, the person responsible for advertising in a small company will probably have to do the best possible with limited resources, which can involve making undesirable compromises. Since many students will be going to work for smaller organizations, they should be fully aware of this distinction.

The range of situations and problems covered in the cases will take students beyond what is normally covered in textbooks. Cases raise topics and issues that are important to people in the advertising business but are not typically dealt with in class. (Agency redundancies are a good example.) They provide a useful way of practicing the exercise of judgment, a critical skill for success in business. They emphasize the uncertainties that abound in the advertising business and the need to be able to deal calmly with unexpected difficulties and situations. And they drive home the message that in spite of the increasing level of sophistication in business, interpersonal relations are still of crucial importance.

Cases will also help students discover that the application of knowledge to a real-life problem is quite different from reproducing it in an essay or multiple choice test. An essential feature of medical education comes when students apply what they have learned to the review of a patient's symptoms, diagnosis of the patient's complaint, and suitable treatment. These cases allow the advertising student to learn in similar fashion.[1]

Some of the cases relate to markets outside the United States. This reflects the fact that the advertising business is becoming more international, not only in terms of big companies mounting global compaigns, but also small companies being encouraged by federal and state governments to increase their sales overseas. In the author's experience, international cases can help build students' confidence by demonstrating that the basic principles of good practice hold good in any market, provided proper allowance is made for local conditions.

With the exception of some cases written to illustrate recurrent or generic problems, all are based on actual organizations and events. In the introduction to the book, it is explained to students that changes were necessary if an organization requested it, or if the author felt they helped in describing people and events with greater candor than would otherwise be possible. The message for students, in other words, is not to regard a case as unrealistic because the company does not exist. In fact, it may be more realistic.

USING THIS MANUAL

The format followed in this manual is intended to provide the instructor with maximum convenience in use. To locate a case on a given topic, turn to the table on page iv, which cross references cases and subjects covered. The cases are not graded in terms of difficulty, since this is a highly subjective judgment and depends on the relative ability and knowledge level of a given class. In general terms, however, the easier cases tend to come earlier in the book.

The notes on the cases have all been prepared to a standard format for ease of reference by the instructor. First comes an analysis of the case written by the case author. This follows the analytical framework explained in the following section and in the introduction to the book. This is followed by suggested questions, which fall into two categories. *Guiding questions* can be used as needed when the instructor wishes to direct students in the appropriate direction. Some students may be able to define the type of problem raised by the case, for example, but others may need a little help. *Discussion questions* concern issues that may not be related directly to the problem in the case, but that can be used to stimulate a fruitful discussion. They might take the case a stage further by introducing a new fact or concept, suggest an alternative perspective, or perhaps raise a broader issue. These questions are intended to be used at the discretion of the instructor, depending on the direction it is desired the class should take.

Three other headings may appear in the notes on a particular case. These are the *actual outcome* (when this can be revealed), *useful references* (when appropriate), and *tips for teaching*.

SUGGESTED FRAMEWORK FOR ANALYSIS

Please note first that this is a suggested framework only. Some instructors will probably have outlines of their own that they would like classes to follow, and so will have no need for this section. For those using the framework, one point must be emphasized at the outset. It is only intended to provide students with a set of broad categories for assembling and analyzing the facts in a case, and the use made of them should be expected to vary according to the type of case and the amount of detail it contains. In some instances there may be nothing to include under a particular category, while in others there may be some important material that does not fit sensibly into any of the existing categories and requires a new one of its own.

The problem with using a framework of this type, as is hinted to students in the introduction to the book, is that it can lead to intellectual laziness. Rather than going to the case with an open mind and assessing the facts on their merits, students tend to approach it framework in hand and look for facts to include under each heading. This saves them thinking about the case, which rather defeats the object of the case study method. It is pointed out in the introduction that this apparent shortcut can also lead them into trouble because it may lead them to overlook an important fact that does not fit neatly under any of the headings, or to misinterpret the relevance of a fact because it has been squeezed into an inappropriate place. In the author's view, students should be encouraged to be as flexible as they wish in terms of the format in which their analysis is presented. The content of the case should always dictate the form of the report, and not the other way round.

The case notes in this manual generally begin with a brief introduction. This is not part of the framework as such, but is included for the benefit of the instructor to give a brief taste of what the case is about. It should tell you something about the kinds of issues raised and make any points the author thinks you should know—for example, whether any particular knowledge is required in order to be able to tackle the case successfully.

The *background or overview* presents the main features of the context in which a decision or recommendation has to be made. It is suggested that students may find it helpful to think of this as a process of focusing down to the issue in question, beginning with the environment and closing down to the field of activity or industry, the organization, its marketing effort, its promotion, and the place of advertising in its promotion mix. This section in particular is likely to vary considerably between cases, according to the amount of information provided, and should be adapted, altered, or perhaps sometimes even ignored.

The *problem statement*, which follows next, should state briefly what students believe to be the point of the case. Sometimes this is fairly obvious (For example, what recommendation should Smith make to the president of his company?). Even so, they may have some difficulty identifying the fundamental nature of Smith's problem. In other instances the type of problem may not be so readily apparent, and students will have to dig for it. In the introduction they are urged to think carefully about the nature of problems. Is a problem actually what people in the case think it is? If there is more than one, are they in some way linked; that is to say, is there a main problem and several subsidiary ones?

The introduction also warns students that defining the problem is the most important part of case analysis. There may well be more than one way of doing so, but if the definition is off target, then so will be the rest of the analysis, because it is based on incorrect assumptions.

Constraints are an important consideration when analyzing any case. Managers do not operate in a vacuum. They work under constraints of time, resources, competitive pressure, and so on. In the light of the way students have defined the problem, what constraints can be deduced from the facts given? Are there any others that common sense suggests may apply?

Decision options are the range of possibilities facing the decision maker. Students should be encouraged not only to look at the obvious ones, but to come up with some creative options of their own. They should be reminded again that advertising takes place in a competitive environment, and that choosing an obvious course of action could play into the hands of a competitor. The instructor should be on the lookout for signs of superficial thinking here, and should probe to make sure that students have really thought through the advantages, disadvantages, and implications of each option.

The *preferred decision* details what is considered the most feasible course of action and gives the rationale for choosing it. Often there will not be any demonstrably "wrong" alternatives that could have disastrous consequences, so students will be choosing among a number of possibilities. On the other hand, some cases confront them with situations in which none of the options have anything to recommend them, and so force the choice of the least undesirable alternative.

The introduction to the book also suggests that students might include a section titled *Further Implications*. This is their opportunity to include any thoughts about the case that have arisen during their analysis but which do not fit in anywhere else. The examples given refer to long term trends, environmental factors and implications for other aspects of the organization's business. It should provide the instructor with a useful indicator of the depth in which the case has been considered and the originality of the thinking that has gone into the analysis.

TEACHING THE CASE CLASS

There are many ways students can learn by the case study method. They can be asked to make individual or group presentations, to produce individual or group reports, to answer written or oral questions in class on prepared cases, to critique the work of others, to play the roles of characters in the case in acting out an important incident, and so on.

From one perspective the choice of method is not important. Case study is intended to stimulate students to approach problems logically and analytically, and this will have been achieved if they have identified the relevant facts, stated the problem clearly, and fully evaluated the options open to them in order to arrive at a recommendation. There is, however, a further benefit to be derived from studying cases. In the introduction to the book it is pointed out that in business it is not enough to be right; you have to be able to convince other people that you are right. There is little point in being able to identify and solve a problem if you cannot persuade those around you that yours is the optimum solution. This is particularly important in advertising management, since the manager's ability to do the job depends on being able to secure the cooperation of other people in the organization. From this perspective, therefore, cases ought to do more than stimulate a student's thought processes. If they are to provide vicarious experience of the advertising world, then elements of persuasion and competition should be built into the class format and evaluation scheme. If students have to fight to have their ideas accepted, and then receive some form of recognition for succeeding, this can help ease their passage from the academic world into the world of business.[2]

The following format was developed by the author to meet this particular need and has been used in case classes for a number of years. It makes no claim to uniqueness. Indeed, others may well have arrived at similar formats prompted by the same needs. However, it has the virtue of forcing students to defend their ideas and to persuade others to accept them, and it does so on three levels: in discussions in small groups; in intergroup competition; and in response to questions from other members of the class. It should be added that the knowledge that their analyses and recommendations are going to come under close scrutiny also motivates students to more thorough and careful preparation. This emphasis on persuasion has been found particularly helpful by students who are naturally shy, or who have had little practice in speaking in public.

At the beginning of the course, the instructor divides the class into an equal number of groups. (The author usually works with ten groups.) The allocation is done on a random basis, trying to ensure that roommates, close friends, etc., are not members of the same group. The cases to be worked on during the semester are identified, dates set, and two groups allocated to each case. The author usually has each group tackle two or three cases, with the remaining class periods being used for lectures, consulting with individual groups, or work on a major term project.

A group is expected to make a class presentation of 15 to 20 minutes on each of its cases and to submit a written report to the instructor. The two groups working on a case are told the perspective from which they should make their presentation—whether they are outside consultants, whether they should assume the role of someone in the case, and so on. The reason for this is not to constrain their freedom of action, but to make certain that they make presentations that are directly comparable.

The object of the verbal presentations is not only to explain the group's conclusions and recommendations to classmates, but to convince them that their group's approach is superior to their opponents'. In other words, the two groups are in direct competition, with the class acting as judges.

At the start of the course the author always encourages students to try new things and to live dangerously in their presentations. This is their great opportunity to do so. If they are going to make mistakes, it is far better they should do so in the classroom than in a situation where it could affect their careers.

When the two presentations have concluded, the members of the class are free to ask questions and elicit any further information they may need to help them reach a decision. This is generally left until both groups have presented, so as not to give an advantage to the second group. It should be said that the extent to which spirited debate ensues depends on everyone having read and thought about the case in advance—something that will probably require periodic reminders from the instructor. At the end of the period of discussion, each group is allowed two minutes to reiterate the main aspects of its presentation, and to deal with any unanswered points that may have arisen. The presenting groups then leave the room, and the rest of the class is asked to decide which of the presentations it found more persuasive. The author does this on a group basis, thus adding one more dimension to the lesson about persuasion. Each group has to reach a consensus and a vote is taken on the basis of one vote per group. In the very rare event of a tie, the deciding vote is cast by the instructor. The winning presenters receive bonus points.

It is recognized that persuasion is a fairly crude measure, but any attempt to isolate presentation skills from content, or to compute scores for component parts, only makes the situation artificial and "academic." Business people listening to an agency pitch or a sales presentation either buy or not, and this is just the kind of setting that the class is trying to simulate.

When the presenting groups come back into the room, the other groups are asked to try and pinpoint what made them vote as they did. The object is to help the presenters improve their presentation skills, so the instructor should try to identify both positive and negative features, in the latter instance without embarrassing the students concerned or undermining their confidence. Comments may reflect the way a presentation was structured ("I found it confusing"), the style or presentation skills ("You went too fast." "I couldn't read your overheads."), or the actual content ("You didn't convince us that we need to spend that much on television." "We felt your assumptions were clearly motivated by male chauvinism."). It is important to keep this discussion as detached and objective as possible, emphasizing to the class that the pupose of the exercise is mutual self-improvement, and that comments are expected to be constructive.

It remains for the instructor to draw the threads together. This is the opportunity to raise options that may not have been considered, mention data that may be open to different interpretation, dissect arguments that do not stand up to close scrutiny, and point to pitfalls that may have trapped the unwary. If the case is being used as a platform from which to begin the exploration of some broader issue, this is the occasion to lead the class in that direction. Great care should be taken, however, not to give students the impression that this is where they are given "the answer."

After the class, the instructor grades the two written reports, looking basically at what they reveal about the two groups' thought processes. How well was the problem defined? Did the group consider the full range of options? Did they really think through the implications of each? Did they progress logically to their preferred option, and did they justify their choice? Does the report contain evidence of original and creative thinking? It is important that the reports, together with appropriate written comments by the instructor, are given back at the next class meeting while details of the case are still relatively fresh in students' minds. In instances where a group may have fared particularly badly, it may be helpful to suggest a meeting in the instructor's office to talk over what went wrong and how performance might be improved.

This format gives the class an "edge," and provides students with a direct incentive to improve their presentation and persuasion skills. Since it is probably rather different from anything they have faced before, it is important to keep emphasizing what is expected of them, and the fact that in this class they "play it for real." Hopefully, by the time they take their final examination they will be thinking less like students and more like managers.

NOTES

1. The importance of reality in advertising education is emphasized by Paul R. Sensbach and Roy D. Adler (1986), "Advertising Courses Should Simulate Real Life," *Journal of Marketing Education* (Spring), 66–70.

2. The benefits of introducing a competitive element into classes are described by Richard M. Sparkman, "Intersectional Competition Sparks Interest in Marketing," *Marketing News* (July 22, 1991), 8.

The Bloomington District*
There's No Merit Badge for Advertising
This Not-For-Profit

FREDERICK B. HOYT

BACKGROUND

Born in Great Britain, Scouting came to the United States in 1911, where it absorbed similar outdoor-focused organizations. Initially for 12–16 year-old males, Boy Scouting has expanded over the last 8 decades to accommodate younger boys as well as teenagers (now 6–18 years old), young adults (boys and girls 14–21), and adult leaders both male and female. Scouting USA, as it renamed itself in the 1980s, better captured the new focus.

The Boy Scout program stresses the delivery of values—character, fitness, leadership, and citizenship—through locally chartered "franchises," extended to local councils (about 400), which then confer yearly charters on existing organizations. "Community and religious organizations and groups, with the help of the BSA," a pamphlet explains, "organize Cub Scout packs, Boy Scout troops, Varsity Scout teams, and Explorer posts for children and youth. They manage these units and control the program of activities so that there is no conflict with the organization's priorities." (BSA Communications Section, Fact Sheet, 1984).

There are a number of organizational structures. First, there are volunteers, both Scouts and adults. The basic building blocks are units—packs, troops, teams, and posts. To implement tactics on an interunit level, and to reach into the community, Scouts use an all-volunteer district committee, headed by a district president. The district committee will handle such matters as membership expansion, running "district" sponsored events such as an annual Scout show, and such matters of common concern as advancement for Eagle (the highest rank). A similar committee exists on the council level. Second, there are paid professionals, such as Don. Generally, depending on the size of the district, or the wealth of the council, there will be only one professional, the district executive, for each district. There will also be a professional staff at the Council level. At the apex is the Council Executive; working for him or her will be several professionals, handling such areas as finance and program, and the various district executives.

PROBLEM

Students are being asked, basically, to address three areas involving a not-for-profit that has never before advertised:

1. What should Don do?

2. What should he stress to the committee?

3. Develop an appropriate campaign and promotional mix.

Constraints

Students will find a number of constraints in the case. First, the organization is not only a not-for-profit which has advertised only minimally in the past, especially at the local level, but also has no budget for advertising or promotion. Second, Don does not control the people who would be making the decisions, at least not in the traditional sense. They are volunteers who work with him, not for him. Third, the decision to develop a promotional mix, consequently, would involve negotiation, influence, and a well-thought-out plan for funding the marketing effort.

Options

There are a number of options which Don could pursue, depending on target market and the amount of money he could raise.

Assuming that he convinces the district committee of the value of advertising, he could then approach the marketing department at the local university for help in mapping a campaign. He might also enlist marketing professionals from among the volunteers. This would lower costs, help assuage some of the doubts his committee seems to have expressed, and perhaps identify the best use of limited resources. For example, a survey might indicate whether or not there was a need for increasing awareness of Scouting in the community. It would require, however, some of Don's already thin time.

What audience is Don trying to reach? If he is working on building the Tiger Cub membership, in the belief that this will reap long-term dividends, he might want to find ways to reach an audience of marrieds with 5–6 year olds. The same might hold for Cub Scouts in general—that is, attract the marrieds with young children. Probably the most effective way would be through television advertising. The local channel carries "The Simpsons," and nearby channels carry cartoons. Television would probably reach more of the target audience in general, though much of the message would get lost in the clutter of advertising. If it were too specific (aimed at parents of Tiger Cubs), most people would ignore it. Television would also be an expensive proposition.

There are also organizational reasons that might impede Don going forward with advertising to this age group: the volunteers on the committee have probably not had much contact with Tiger Cubs, and from some of the comments, have not thoroughly embraced the wisdom of integrating backwards.

If he looks to enlist Boy Scout-age youth, either television or radio might be feasible. MTV—which would reach the segment—would have negative connotations with his committee of adults; most of the stations that would reach teenagers would probably bear a similar stigma.

If he seeks to build awareness of adults in his district, he could probably use any of the media he considered, including newspaper or classifieds. However, reaching parents of 11 year olds or older might not be effective in enlisting their children. Furthermore, newspaper material would not convey the excitement of the outdoors, which is an important part of Scouting.

PREFERRED DECISION

Given the "introductory stage" of marketing in this not-for-profit, Don might do best by going slowly—enlisting support from his committee to seek assistance from the local university or professional marketers. That would have the advantage of building support for the idea, while at the same time minimizing the cost. A calculated introduction could leave the committee the opportunity to monitor both costs and effectiveness.

If Don's "personal selling" activities are primarily aimed at increasing the membership in the Tiger Cubs, as seems evident in the statistics, then the advertising campaign ought to supplement his activities. Limited funds might best be committed to focusing on parents of 5–6 year olds.

QUESTIONS
Guiding Questions

An important question in this case is, "Who is the target market?" Is it the "ultimate consumer?" Or is it more important to reach the parent as gatekeeper?

Another question might be the message of the advertisement. Should it be directed to increase the awareness of Scouting in general. How can that be accomplished if the product mix is diverse. Tiger Cubs are not the same as Explorers, for example. Can there be "family brand" advertisements, or must they be "individual brand"?

Finally, how can Don convince his committee of the value of diverting scarce resources to an untested method?

Questions for Discussion

The case permits and in fact encourages a discussion of the value of advertising in not-for-profits. The reluctance of the Scout volunteers to permit advertising is not uncommon in many service industries, such as law or medicine. In the case of not-for-profits, one could even go further and ask whether advertising per se harms their image. If a company underwrites advertising for a not-for-profit and so indicates, does that contaminate the not-for-profit?

WHAT REALLY HAPPENED

The material presented in this case is relatively close to the decision which faced a local council in central Illinois. The council itself assigned one of its professionals to develop a volunteer committee to evaluate the need for advertising. The committee in turn contacted a local university, where a class conducted focus groups and a phone survey. The results indicated, to the surprise of both professionals and volunteers, a low recognition of Boy Scouting in the community. The marketing committee accordingly sought to increase awareness of Scouting in the community through advertising on three radio stations which appeal to different segments. The most money is committed to a contemporary rock station. This committee is currently monitoring the radio commercials in order to evaluate their effectiveness.

CASE 2

Fanstone's Funeral Homes*

Terence Nevett

INTRODUCTION

There are indications of a growing resentment among consumers about the use of the telephone for promotional purposes. This medium becomes particularly controversial when used to promote professional services, and even more so when the services are those of a funeral director.

BACKGROUND

Fanstone's Funeral Homes, an old established and well respected local firm, uses the telephone to promote their range of services. Calls are made by members of the firm and emphasize the benefits of preplanning to meet a family's funeral expenses. Mrs. Harrison, who has just lost her son, receives such a call, and takes strong exception.

PROBLEM STATEMENT

Were Fanstone's correct in their response to Mrs. Harrison's reaction?

Constraints

- Mrs. Harrison's emotional state following her recent bereavement
- Mrs. Harrison's attitude, having seen funeral directors' ads in the hospital
- Fanstone's regular use of the telephone for promotion

- Entrenched positions on both sides
- Mrs. Harrison unlikely to begin preplanning for another funeral at this time

Decision Options

The first caller could have apologized and terminated the conversation. That would have done nothing to retrieve the situation, but would have limited the damage. Alternatively, Mark Fanstone could have apologized and then terminated the conversation. This would have conveyed an impression of deeper regret on the firm's part, in addition to limiting damage. The option chosen by Mark Fanstone was to try to justify the firm's use of the telephone by explaining its advantages. If he had been able to do this successfully, it would have projected an image of a firm that was both caring and efficiently managed. However, he only succeeded in upsetting Mrs. Harrison even more. Since she was expecting a further apology, it was hardly tactful to solicit congratulations.

PREFERRED OPTION

Mark Fanstone seems to have had little to gain from prolonging the conversation with Mrs. Harrison. It is true that Mrs. Harrison's recent loss of her son did not, in theory, preclude her as a prospect for preplanned funerals. However, the great advantage of the telephone over other media is that it provides feedback, enabling the communicator to adjust the message to the needs of the individual audience member. In this instance, the sensitivity of the issue was surely apparent, indicating that Mrs. Harrison had effectively removed herself from the market for the time being. Fanstone's should have recognized this and extricated themselves from the situation as quickly as possible. Mark Fanstone's approach was tactless under the circumstances and seems to have led to negative word-of-mouth communication.

QUESTIONS
Guiding Questions

What is the main advantage of the telephone as a medium?

Was the initial caller's response reasonable?

What were the choices facing Mark Fanstone?

Evaluate Mark Fanstone's approach when speaking to Mrs. Harrison.

Evaluate Mrs. Harrison's response: (a) to the first caller; (b) to Mark Fanstone.

Discussion Questions

Is the telephone a suitable medium for promoting funeral services?

In Britain, funeral directors are not allowed to advertise on television or radio. Why do you think this is? Would you want to see a similar ban introduced in the United States?

Should funeral services be advertised with cut-price or discount claims? In hospitals?

Are there differences between advertising funeral homes and advertising other professional services?

TEACHING SUGGESTIONS

Although this note has been written from the viewpoint of the advertiser, it can equally be approached from the consumer's perspective. Students can be asked to imagine themselves in Mrs. Harrison's position and to think how they would have felt. Some of the class may have relevant experiences of their own to contribute. The discussion can be broadened to include such topics as random digit dialing and the use of recorded messages, and possible abuses that may occur because the message is confidential and does not exist in permanent form. The instructor may also care to raise the subject of what media students think funeral homes should or should not be allowed to use.

The characters of Mrs. Harrison and Mark Fanstone, in addition to the views they hold, are well suited to role-play.

CASE 3

Angela's Flowers on Fourth*

Terence Nevett

INTRODUCTION

Sometimes the importance of advertising to a business can be such that it is a crucial factor in "go – no go" decisions. This case asks students to think about the role of advertising in the floral trade, and for one florist's shop in particular, and to consider what constitutes reasonable expectations and limitations.

BACKGROUND

Angela Devine is enthusiastic about flowers and has worked for several florists. Her academic background includes both business subjects and those related directly to floristry. Her experiences have led her to be less enthusiastic about the trade itself, and she regards florists as conservative and inefficient. When she is offered the chance to purchase Flowers on Fourth, her father promises to provide financial backing if she is convinced the operation will be profitable.

Features of the trade are given in Angela's SWOT analysis. Note that florists tend to have greater expertise in the selection and handling of flowers and are still the main source for consumers who are buying flowers as gifts. However, the trade generally seems very conservative in outlook. Advertising has remained concentrated on gift-giving occasions, and floral offerings consist mainly of traditional varieties of flowers and traditional floral designs. Now florists are facing stiff price competition from other sources on their most profitable lines.

8

PROBLEM STATEMENT

Are Angela's expectations about what advertising could achieve for her business reasonable and realistic?

Constraints

These are applicable to the floral business generally:

- Image of the trade as perceived by consumers
- Declining consumer interest in "traditional" flowers
- Increasing competition from nontraditional outlets, especially on price

Constraints applicable in Angela's case specifically

- Image currently projected by Flowers on Fourth
- Limitations to the power of one outlet to counter unfavorable consumer perceptions of the trade generally
- Reliance on family funding: insufficient to permit Angela to introduce a new name and concept for the business and also undertake extensive advertising

Decision Options

Angela can buy Flowers on Fourth, change the name to Devine Flowers, and convert it to a different type of florist business. She could then use advertising to distance her store from the conservatively perceived mass of traditional florists.

Another option would be to take over Flowers on Fourth as a going concern and either keep the same identity (while perhaps making some improvements to the stock assortment) or make very gradual changes to the identity to try and retain existing customers as well as attracting new ones.

A third option is not to buy the store at all and either to look for something nearer to her own conception of how a florist's business ought to be run or to seek a different kind of career.

PREFERRED DECISION

The choice is really governed by two factors: what advertising could be expected to achieve for Angela, and the future for the floral business generally. Environmental trends seem broadly favorable to the sale of flowers, but the traditional florists do not seem well positioned to take advantage of them. The image of floristry needs to be improved, and this requires consistent advertising of a type and intensity that florists so far have not undertaken. In order for Angela to achieve something like this on her own, she would probably have to create a separate identity for her store that would distinguish her in consumers' minds both from the traditional type of florist and from alternative outlets such as supermarkets.

This would be a difficult task for any small retailer. For someone with no experience in advertising, and by implication unable to afford the services of an agency, it is surely asking too much. In addition, Angela's plans for Devine Flowers include turning the buying of flowers into a routine purchase. This is too much for a single retailer to accomplish, though it might be a realistic long-term objective for the whole trade.

Given the circumstances of the case, there seems no way of using research to determine whether the Devine Flowers concept would keep Flowers on Fourth's existing customer base, attract new customers, or increase the frequency of purchase. A decision not to proceed with the purchase of the business would therefore be reasonable. If students feel strongly that she should go ahead, then she should introduce any changes gradually so as to minimize the risk of alienating existing customers.

QUESTIONS
Guiding Questions

Is Angela expecting too much of advertising?

What are the pros and cons of changing the name of the business?

Would it be possible to promote flowers as a routine purchase in such a way that the campaign did not also help supermarkets?

Discussion Questions

Can flowers be promoted to consumers in the same way as other products?

What determines where consumers buy flowers?

How important a consideration is price when buying flowers?

Is Angela overestimating consumer knowledge of flowers and floral designs?

In the longer term, how great is the threat to florists from alternative kinds of gifts to mark special occasions? If it is significant, could it be countered by advertising?

CASE 4

B.I. Cycles of Madras, India*

KARTIK PASHUPATI

INTRODUCTION

The B.I. Cycles of India case deals primarily with the issue of whether or not to change the creative strategy for Ulysses Captain bicycles in the light of the greater availability of television, which now enables children (the intended users) to be targeted in addition to the parents (the decision makers). The Ulysses Captain problem situation is preceded by a brief case history of the previous successful launch by the same company (and ad agency) of the MXA SLR, a bicycle targeted to a different subculture within the same country.

While no previous background on the part of the students is assumed with regard to their knowledge of the Indian market or with respect to international advertising, it is important to sensitize them to issues such as the substantial difference that exists in the manner in which bicycles are perceived and used in most Asian (especially Third World) countries compared to the United States. The MXA SLR case is presented first in order to emphasize this point. A brief study of the development of commercial television in India would also be useful in understanding the finer aspects of the case. Finally, a map of India, preferably in conjunction with the linguistic differences in various states/regions would also aid in a better understanding of the case.

BACKGROUND/OVERVIEW

Bicycles in India, as in most Asian countries, are viewed primarily as utilitarian transportation for those who cannot afford mopeds, scooters, or motorcycles. (Cars are well beyond the reach of the majority of the middle class.) This is in sharp contrast with the situation in the U.S. and many other developed countries, where bicycles are viewed as hobby or leisure vehicles by a substantial proportion of the target market. As indicated in the case, the industry is competitive, and India is home to some of the world's largest bicycle manufacturers, such as Hero Cycles, based in Punjab. Most bicycle advertising has hitherto been targeted toward the lower middle-class working male, using mainly print and outdoor media.

In such a context, B.I. Cycles has successfully launched a niche product—the MXA SLR—targeted toward big-city teenagers, whose perception and usage of bicycles does not quite fit the mold of the lower middle-class male. The entire marketing mix for the MXA SLR, from the product down to the advertising, reflects the fact that this is a product targeted to a different subculture—one that is influenced substantially by Western values and lifestyles. The use of English as the primary language for advertising the MXA SLR also points toward this fact. The target users of the MXA SLR could be addressed directly through a variety of audio-visual media.

B.I. has now launched the Ulysses Captain, also a bicycle targeted at school-going children, but those belonging to a different subculture. (The fact that the Captain was launched as a brand extension of Ulysses was intended to capitalize on the goodwill that the Ulysses brand had with the father, who was presumably a bicycle user himself.) Apart from the differences in subculture, television coverage was not available for this segment, thus leading to the decision to target the parent (primarily the male parent). However, rapid developments in the media environment have made it possible for B.I. to address the end user (the schoolkid) directly through television, in addition to the decision maker (the parent). Television has also made it possible to reach many more mothers who may not have been exposed to the print media due to limited female literacy.

PROBLEM STATEMENT

The decision issue, very simply, is whether B.I. Cycles should accept the advertising agency's suggestion to target parents and children with a television campaign using a primarily musical/emotional appeal (which also shows the ruggedness of the Ulysses Captain) or request a more "cognitive" approach targeting only parents.

Constraints

Although no specific budget figures are mentioned in the case, both advertiser and agency appear to agree that B.I. Cycles cannot afford two separate campaigns using different appeals. The different characteristics of television and print media and the differences in subcultures, as well as the linguistic complications involved in addressing the different regions, also need to be considered while analyzing the case. (In this context, it is worth pointing out that advertising jingles have been successfully adapted across various languages, by altering just the lyrics while keeping the music the same.)

Decision Options

The following are a few of the decision options available to B.I. Cycles:

Accept the advertising agency's suggestions and proceed with the jingle-based commercial for Captain

Request the agency to present a new television commercial featuring more cognitive appeals, directed primarily at the parent

Use the jingles on television and use print media (such as regional language magazines) to target parents with cognitive appeals

Continue using print media alone, perhaps with greater outdoor media support as a reminder

PREFERRED DECISION

By not using a television campaign directed at children themselves, B.I. would be losing out on an opportunity to address the actual user of the product. While schoolkids in the smaller towns (the target market) admittedly do not hold the purse strings and also do not exercise as strong an influence over the brand decision as urban teenagers, it is possible that the impact of television (through its mere availability) might change the latter fact. Any decision that B.I. Cycles makes must, therefore, include the agency's suggestion. Thus, either option 1 or 3 could be favored, depending on the resources available.

GUIDANCE/DISCUSSION QUESTIONS

N.B.: Some of the following questions have been framed to broaden the scope of the discussion/analysis that is possible using this case as an illustrative example:

Discuss the differences in the uses (and perceptions) of bicycles between the Indian context, and your own market. What are the implications of these differences in terms of (a) the marketing mix, (b) creative strategy and appeals, and (c) media strategy?

The case presents two different subcultures in the Indian bicycle market: the big city subculture (MXA SLR), and the small-town subculture (Ulysses Captain). Identify two or three such subcultures in your own country and analyze the impact of the differences in these subcultures in terms of (a) the marketing mix, (b) creative strategy and appeals, and (c) media strategy for any product category which you consider relevant.

What are the different ways in which advertisers can tackle the problems of advertising in a diversity of languages?

The case discusses the potential impact that the introduction of television can have on creative strategy. Discuss how the introduction of new communication technologies (such as telemarketing, interactive telephones, cable television, etc.) have impacted marketing communications strategies in your own markets.

The screening of commercials in movie theaters was used as the primary audio-visual medium for the advertising of the MXA SLR before the availability of commercial television. The theatrical screening of commercials is making a comeback in the U.S. market. What are the environmental conditions that are contributing to this comeback?

What are the creative and media strategy recommendations for the Ulysses Captain campaign that you would make to the executives at B.I. Cycles?

CASE 5

Englander Advertising Agency*

TERENCE NEVETT

INTRODUCTION

In addition to the kinds of "textbook" decisions students are normally called upon to make in class, managing in the advertising business also involves making decisions about people. Sometimes this can involve tough choices. This case concerns the issues that have to be faced by the management of an advertising agency that has just lost a major account and has to face the prospect of terminating some of its employees.

BACKGROUND

Agencies have been growing generally leaner, handling increased billings with fewer staff. Englander Advertising, with 193 staff, has lost an account worth $25 million of its $115 million billings. Employees account for 65 percent of operating costs. The rule of thumb is to cut one person for every $1 million in lost billings, so that Englander has to think of cutting about 25 people.

PROBLEM STATEMENT

The situation has to be resolved in two stages. First, does the agency cut now or try to replace the lost business? Second, if the cuts are made now (or indeed have to be made later), where should the ax fall?

Constraints

- The effect on Englander's financial position if staff who worked on the lost account are retained (The case does not contain detailed financial information, so students can only discuss this point in general terms.)

- The loss of specialist knowledge if those employees are terminated

- The attitudes of Thomas and Walser

Decision Options

The affected staff could be retained for the time being while the agency goes after new business. This would help preserve the family atmosphere in the agency and sustain morale. It would also keep together those people with expertise in the cosmetics area, thus providing a springboard for the agency to go after a new cosmetics client. Against this, and in favor of immediate cuts, it can be argued that employees would fear eventual redundancy anyway, and this would have an unfortunate effect on morale. The uncertainty would start them job hunting, and that would probably mean that the best people would be the ones to leave the agency, because they would find it easier to find new jobs. Those who had to be cut eventually would, in one way, have been treated unfairly, because they may have missed out on new job opportunities. In addition, keeping those people on would damage agency profitability.

The options on where to cut consist of senior or lower level staff. Cuts at the top would involve fewer people and would leave the "engine room" of the agency intact so that the efficient handling of accounts would be unaffected. On the other hand, preserving senior people would reassure current and potential clients. Those at the top are also more likely to have important contacts that are necessary if the agency is to attract new business. The argument for cutting lower level staff is that there is a greater chance of identifying jobs that are not directly productive. However, this could leave the agency top-heavy.

PREFERRED DECISION

This depends on the criteria employed. If the chief consideration is maintaining profits, then Walser is right to cut now. However, an agency really cannot be treated in the same way as a manufacturing unit. It consists of a volatile collection of individuals living a stressful and insecure lifestyle. Morale is an important factor in keeping the creative drive at its peak, and this represents a key element of agency management. From this perspective, it might be better to keep the affected staff for the time being. A prospective client looking at an agency's previous work in a given field may well want to meet the people involved. Englanders would be in an unfortunate position if they had to admit that those concerned had been terminated.

Thomas might consider setting some kind of deadline by which the lost business must be replaced and making those who previously worked on the cosmetic account primarily responsible. In that way, their fate would be largely in their own hands, and they would have a strong motivation to succeed.

As regards where to cut if it becomes necessary, the least unsatisfactory answer seems to be some form of compromise, taking people from both senior and lower levels. Both Thomas and Walser make valid points—there would be little sense in an organization top-heavy with generals at the expense of the troops, but at the same time, there must be some unproductive jobs at lower levels in the agency that could be cut without the effects being too serious. There is no such thing as a best way to make cuts. The manager must try to inflict the least damage possible on the organization, while balancing this against whatever obligations are felt to those concerned as individuals.

QUESTIONS
Guiding Questions

How important is an agency's collective expertise in a given area of business?

In what ways does managing an advertising agency differ from managing a manufacturing business?

How can financial considerations be balanced against personal feelings in the case?

Discussion Questions

To what extent, if any, should Thomas consider the personal circumstances of individual employees when deciding whether to terminate them?

An obvious target for redundancy has a wife who is eight months pregnant. If you terminate him he loses medical insurance. Should this affect your choice?

Could you (student) call 25 people into your office just before Christmas, among them a number of old friends and people you have known for years, and tell them they are terminated?

TEACHING SUGGESTION

The characters of Walser and Thomas can be seen as representing the logical and the emotional, the financial and the humane, the short and long term. The case is thus well suited to presentation in the form of a debate. Two teams or two individual students can be asked to represent the views of Walser and Thomas respectively. The class can generate considerable student involvement, especially if the others are asked to take the part of Englander employees, including those whose jobs are under threat.

CASE 6

Revlon Cosmetics Advertising

JOHN M. SCHLEEDE

INTRODUCTION

In this case the turbulent cosmetic industry is profiled. Changing demographics and increased competition have created a major problem for former market leader Revlon. Although the basic issue presented to the student in the case is media strategy, the broader issues of positioning and basic promotional strategy must be settled first.

OVERVIEW

Consumer behavior: Although little information is given about consumer behavior directly, the behaviors of the competitors in the industry suggest how they believe consumers make their purchase decisions. The following chart summarizes this information.

Distribution Method/ Brand	Product Class	Promotion Strategy	Decision Process
Mass merchandisers/ (eg. Cover Girl)	Convenience good	Advertising/ self service	Low involvement Inertial brand loyalty
Department stores/ (eg. Estee Lauder)	Shopping good	Advertising, promotions, POP selling	High involvement Moderate brand loyalty
Direct distribution/ (eg. Mary Kay)	Specialty good	Personal selling	High involvement High brand loyalty

The relative success of some brands in each of these categories suggests that there are in fact three distinct consumer segments. It is interesting to note that Revlon is attempting to compete in two of these segments simultaneously with the same brand name and promotional strategy. This has undoubtedly contributed to their decline, as their department store image is damaged by their mass merchandiser line, while the resources have not been there to support a strictly mass marketing approach.

A second factor that students should discern from the case is that the relative sizes of the segments are changing. Avon's decreasing market share and the slowdown in department store sales growth suggest that more consumers view cosmetics as a convenience good. Old brand loyalties are declining and sales promotions have become increasingly important.

Competition: It would probably be best for students to consider the competition within the context of the three segments presented earlier. The following chart might summarize the market positions that the student might use.

Segment	Market Leader	Challengers	Followers
Mass merchandisers	Cover Girl	Maybelline	Clarion, Revlon, Max Factor
Department stores	Estee Lauder	Clinique, Lancômb	Revlon, Elizabeth Arden, Faberge
Direct marketers	Avon	Mary Kay	

Revlon is far from being the market leader and might best be characterized as a follower. The leaders in both of the first two segments are currently leading not only in market share but also in promotional spending. The challengers compete closely in all aspects including market share, distribution penetration, and promotional spending. More importantly, they aspire to be the market leader. At least from the information presented in the case, it should be noted by the student that Revlon does *not* fit either of these categories and is seemingly content to be a follower. They *do* spend a lot of money, but the expenditures are spread over a plethora of products in two distinct segments.

Other Considerations:

1. Changing demographics which have changed the growth rates of different product lines

   color cosmetics—low growth
   fragrances—no growth
   skin care—high growth

2. Increasing consolidation of the industry which might conclude in a shift from monopolistic competition to oligopoloy

3. Changing promotional strategies
       mass merchandisers using television advertising
       department store brands moving from media to promotions

PROBLEM STATEMENT

The case presents the student with the task of developing an appropriate media strategy. First, however, the student must decide, based on the available evidence, how Revlon should be positioned. This decision affects the selection of the promotional mix, the role of advertising, and finally the creative and media strategies.

Constraints

The major constraints presented in the case are environmental and were discussed earlier. However, there are two other internal factors which the student should consider. First, Revlon has been marketed successfully for many years with its current name and position. A radical change in direction is probably not possible without damaging its reputation with current customers. Secondly, resources are limited over the long term. Unless the selected strategy can deliver an immediate payback, there will not be the resources to continue the campaign. Obviously the strategy chosen must be results oriented.

Decision Options

1. Toward which market should Revlon position itself?
   Assuming that Revlon has no desire to move to direct distribution, the company has three options:
   Continue as before, aiming at two markets.
   Focus on the mass market.
   Focus on the department store market.

Mass Market

Advantages:

1. Mass market is twice as large as the department store market.

2. Mass market is the fastest growing market.

3. Revlon is currently strong in the mass market (15 percent share).

Disadvantages:

1. P&G and other major competitors spend large sums on advertising that would be difficult for Revlon to match.

2. Revlon doesn't have the expertise of P&G in mass marketing.

Department Store Market

1. Less money would be required in promotion than in the mass market.	1. With the entrance of Unilever, another tough new competitor has been added.
2. Market is likely to remain large.	2. Revlon's share in this market is relatively small.

Both Markets

1. They are currently competing in both markets.	1. This creates confusion with their brand image.
	2. It requires additional investment to compete in both markets.

Based on this analysis, it could be argued that the mass market has the most potential for Revlon. Even though P&G is a tough competitor, so is Estee Lauder, and the addition of Unilever will make this a difficult market to crack. The department store market is smaller and is not growing as rapidly as the mass market. Number-two brand in the mass market, Maybelline, is vulnerable, and Schering Plough has been looking for someone to purchase this line. Finally, Cover Girl's image as a "cheaper, younger" cosmetic can be exploited by Revlon. Revlon has an excellent, if stodgy reputation, and good promotion can exploit this opportunity.

2. What should the promotion mix be?

The mass market was characterized earlier as a low involvement learning situation. The decision process might best be characterized as follows:

Awareness of the brand

Trial purchase

Relative satisfaction

Repurchase

Revlon already has high awareness; however, a case can be made that Cover Girl and Maybelline have significantly higher top-of-the-mind awareness. Trial is likely to have occurred as well. There is no evidence to suggest dissatisfaction with the product's performance. It does not follow that substantial brand loyalty exists, however. In low involvement learning, brand loyalty is likely to be relatively low and repurchase patterns easily disrupted. Consumers might view Revlon as one of a number of acceptable brands.

If this is the case, Revlon needs to develop a more packaged-goods type promotional mix. Heavy advertising expenditures will be required to develop and maintain top-of-the-mind awareness and to reinforce satisfaction. Consumer promotion will be needed to drive trials and repurchase. Success in this strategy will also require a substantial investment in trade promotion to insure adequate distribution and reseller support.

3. What media strategy should Revlon use?

The research in the case shows that heavy users of color cosmetics tend to be heavy magazine readers and light television viewers. The department store brands have capitalized on this and on the high involvement nature of the decision by using all magazines. Cover Girl and Maybelline, recognizing the low involvement nature of the decision, have balanced the more efficient media class, magazines, with the more intrusive television.

Revlon has two choices: copy the competition or avoid them. Going head to head will require a substantial investment in media expenditures. If Cover Girl and Maybelline fight back, as is likely, Revlon will not be able to match their expenditures. Therefore an avoidance strategy would seem to make sense.

Radio, newspapers, and outdoor would not be appropriate as a primary media class for Revlon. The use of color, the image orientation, and the necessity for national mass (yet selective) coverage would argue against these. A better choice would be to put media expenditures into cable and syndicated television. Cable stations such as Lifetime and syndicated programs such as the "Oprah Winfrey Show" would deliver the target audience with relatively little waste, good cost efficiency, and almost no direct competition. Coop advertising with retailers would provide a second important element in the promotional mix.

CASE 7

Meds Tampons in Australia

TERENCE NEVETT

INTRODUCTION

In this case students are asked to make the decision that faced the marketing manager of Johnson & Johnson in Australia. It involves the kind of situation that is dreaded by everyone involved in creating and planning an advertising campaign: an original and perhaps provocative creative approach stimulated tremendous hostility on the part of certain consumers, bringing with it the threat of a boycott of all the company's products. The case can also be used to introduce a discussion of the role of self regulation, and in particular whether the regulatory authorities should be involved in making judgments on matters of taste, although these topics are not dealt with directly.

BACKGROUND

Johnson & Johnson is a multinational company marketing consumer, pharmaceutical, and professional products in 155 countries. In March 1989, J & J in Australia launched a new campaign for Meds tampons. The innovative campaign had been prepared by J & J's agency, Ogilvy and Mather, after extensive research. Its appearance was greeted by a public outcry and a threat to boycott all the company's products.

24

PROBLEM STATEMENT

Fred Vermeer, J & J's marketing manager, has to decide whether to withdraw the new compaign.

Constraints

The constraints include:

- Time: Vermeer facing a threatened boycott

- Broader implications for J & J: all the company's products under threat, including a number of market leaders

- Character of J & J: typically a conservative company, proud of its reputation in the pharmaceutical and professional fields

Decision Options

Ride out the storm:

- Complaints may be coming from vocal minority.

- Majority of complainants were older women who were not part of the target audience.

- Research showed the campaign was accepted by younger women at whom it was targeted.

- Complaints about the campaign had been rejected by the Advertising Council.

- Sales of Meds had risen since the campaign broke.

Withdraw the campaign:

- The controversy may be damaging J & J's other interests—it is not the kind of company to benefit from this kind of publicity.

- The boycott could have widespread repercussions in all J & J's markets.

- The problem would be resolved quickly and with minimal damage.

It is important to note that the creative approach employed in the ads seems so novel that there does not seem to be any possibility of compromise. There is no way it could have been toned down to satisfy the objections raised against it and still have retained anything of its original character.

PREFERRED OPTION

The case can be argued either way. While it is hard on a point of principle to concede to a loud-mouthed minority who are not even potential purchasers of the product, the benefit to the company from increased sales of Meds has to be weighed against possible losses in other markets if the boycott is really effective.

QUESTIONS
Guiding Questions

What could be the implications for J & J if the campaign is not withdrawn?

Identify any elements of the campaign that might be considered offensive. Whom are they likely to offend?

Does the fact that complaints have been rejected by Australia's Advertising Council mean that J & J would be at fault by withdrawing the campaign?

Discussion Questions

What do students feel would be the reaction to such a campaign in the United States?

Should self regulation of advertising extend to matters of taste?

Is a boycott of all a company's products a valid means of consumer protest about the advertising for one of them?

Do students feel this case raises any ethical, moral, or religious issues?

WHAT ACTUALLY HAPPENED

J & J withdrew the campaign. In Vermeer's view, the adverse reaction was so strong that he had no alternative.

REFERENCE

There is brief coverage in Geoffrey Lee Martin, "Australians Blast Tampon Ads," *Advertising Age* (March 27, 1989), 34. It is not recommended that this be given to students since it reports Vermeer's decision.

CASE 8

Huggies Pull – Ups®

MARTHA ROGERS

INTRODUCTION

The Huggies Pull – Ups case is a new-product introduction (actually a product extension) in a very competitive consumer packaged-good category. The case can serve as an examination of media and promotion, creative, or a complete campaign. Proposals for follow-up research would also be appropriate.

BACKGROUND AND OVERVIEW

Kimberly – Clark is a company that is only one-fourth the size of P&G. Furthermore, K – C spends $9 million per year less than P&G on mass media advertising for disposable diapers. Although the amount of money spent on advertising for disposable diapers is well documented, several changes facing branded packaged goods will have an impact on this case:

1. The growing disillusionment with Free Standing Inserts (FSIs) as an effective medium for coupon distribution will lead to more direct distribution of promotions to consumers, especially with such an identifiable market (mothers with toddler-age children).

2. Advertising is shrinking as a proportion of promotion dollars spent. This may be especially true of push-strategy efforts such as slotting fees, etc.

3. Introduction of new products will require ever-greater investments over maintaining image, in the face of increasing ad clutter.

PROBLEM STATEMENT

What is at issue in this case is the introduction of a new product by the second-place manufacturer in the parent category. The decisions to be made center on the issue of primary demand (since the idea of disposable training pants is a new one) vs. selective demand (since the success of Kimberly–Clark's Pull–Ups will probably lead very soon to competition from Procter & Gamble).

QUESTIONS AND ISSUES

Kimberly–Clark successfully introduced a product extension with a minimum of cannibalization. Questions facing the creative department have centered on the future distinction between primary-demand vs. selective-demand advertising objectives as well as positioning the product to withstand the inevitable onslaught from Procter & Gamble.

Should the disposable training pant be positioned as an alternative to disposable diapers or as an alternative to other training pants?

Should advertising for Pull–Ups continue the "Happy Baby" theme used by Huggies for over a decade to a "Happy Child" approach? Or should the focus of the ads be on the beleaguered parents? What are the best media to use to reach the prospects?

Given that Kimberly–Clark is a company that is only one-fourth the size of P&G, and that K–C spends $9 million per year less than P&G on mass-media advertising for diapers, how can K–C maximize their advertising dollars against Pampers and Luvs?

What sales promotion efforts, if any, should K–C use for Huggies?

How can the first-entry position of Huggies be capitalized?

Since gender-specific brands were popularized by Pampers in the mid-1980s (blue for boys, pink for girls—with zoned protection), consumers have responded well. How should Huggies handle a competitive offering by P&G of gender-specific disposable training pants?

How should Huggies handle the environmental issue?

PREFERRED DECISIONS

Primary vs. Secondary: Huggies must maintain strong Huggies identification right from the start.

Positioning: Pull–Ups should be positioned as an alternative to disposable diapers during the toilet training process.

Basic creative decision: Although the "right" decision is not definable, some basic guidelines might include making sure the creative for Huggies Pull–Ups focuses on the child feeling all grown up by the toilet training process. Shifting the focus from the beleaguered parents to the happy child is more positive, since parents would prefer to believe they are toilet training their child for the child's good and not for their own convenience.

Media To Use: An examination of secondary resources such as MRI, Simmons, etc., reveals the best market for this product to be two-fold: working mothers and stay-at-home mothers almost equally. This means that daytime TV will be economical but will only reach half the market. Prime-time network TV as well as cable TV (notably Lifetime and Nickelodeon) will reach working mothers as will magazines geared to the two lifestyles. Direct marketing, already used by P&G and K – C for new mothers, should be used to distribute coupons and tout the advantages of happy toilet training.

Maximizing media dollars: Huggies must use the well-liked and familiar Huggies name to promote Pull – Ups. The objective must be to make *Huggies* synonymous with disposable training pants.

Sales promotions: New mothers are particularly promotion-responsive. Possible promotions could include *train* sets or toys to be sold as self-liquidating premiums, as well as *train* trip sweepstakes. Cross-brand tie-ins may prove useful, such as coupons or samples for Pull – ups with the purchase of Gerry potty seats.

Gender-specific competition: This is a tough question. Students may come up with many different right answers, but should demonstrate awareness that offering gender-specific products as well as the non-gender "white"—in several sizes—has the positive effect of increasing shelf frontage in the store, thus making a bigger Huggies (or P&G) impact than the single offering can. But it also will require bigger slotting fees and more persuasion for supermarket managers to devote so much space to these products—managers who are already overwhelmed with twice as many different products as were available less than ten years ago.

Environmental concerns: Huggies must be more vocal about their efforts.

TEACHING TIPS

The greatest challenge for traditional students with this case is to understand what parents and very young children are going through. Focus groups will help them better understand the toilet-training process, and the role the various competitive products can play. It's probably useful to have a package of the actual product on hand for students to examine—available in the grocery store near the disposable diapers.

REFERENCES

Jefferson, David (1990). "Diaper Marker Turns PR Crisis into Sales Opportunity," *Wall Street Journal*, February 7.

Freeman, Laurie (1989). "Huggies Adds to Line with Training Pants," *Advertising Age*, April 10, 69.

——(1990). "Diaper Image Damaged: Poll," *Advertising Age*, July 9, 46.

Miller, Annette (1989). "A Pitched Battle for Baby's Bottom," *Newsweek*, March 6, 44.

Samuelson, Robert J. (1990). "The Great Diaper Debate," *Reader's Digest*, August, 119–120.

——(1990). "The Way We Diaper," *Newsweek*, March 19, 46.

Schiller, Zachary (1990). "Turning Pampers into Plant Food," *Business Week*, October 22, 38–9.

Simmons (1988). *Study of Media and Markets*, Vol. P–29, "Games and Toys, Children's and Baby Apparel and Specialty Products."

Wall Street Journal (1989). "Diaper Derby Heats Up as Firms Add Color, Frills," May 9, B1.

——(1989). "Even Environmentalists Still Use Disposable Diapers," December 26, B1.

——(1990). "Weyerhauser Unveils Hybrid Diaper Brand," January 26, B1.

CASE 9

Harry H. Gubbard, D.D.S.*

TERENCE NEVETT

INTRODUCTION

This case is intended to provide the instructor with a base from which to introduce students to some of the issues that arise when members of the professions advertise. The format of this note has been modified accordingly.

Advertising by members of professions is a relatively recent phenomenon. In the minds of some consumers—and some professional people—it remains an undesirable practice and serves as an indication that the advertiser is unable to attract business by other more "legitimate" means. The details presented here reflect the attitudes and beliefs of a real-life dentist whose identity has been changed for professional reasons.

BACKGROUND

Professional advertising has been permitted since 1977, when the Supreme Court ruled that it was protected under the First Amendment.

A survey conducted in Oregon showed that the more recently a dentist graduated, the more favorable he or she is likely to be towards advertising. This is probably because older dentists tend to have established practices and so do not have the same need to advertise. These older dentists are also likely to hold senior positions in the various professional organizations.

Dr. Gubbard is considering advertising more aggressively and is having to confront his own prejudices. Other dentists in the area are apparently using advertising with some success.

PROBLEM STATEMENT

Should Dr. Gubbard advertise? If so, what message and media strategies should he employ?

Constraints

Constraints include:

- Dr. Gubbard's own attitude to advertising: he would approach it with considerable misgivings.

- Aggressive advertising will offend the dental establishment.

- The State Dental Association's *Code of Professional Conduct* limits claims that dentists can make in advertisements.

- Dr. Gubbard's own ad in the Yellow Pages probably has not generated any new patients.

Preferred Decision

In view of his own misgivings about advertising and his worries about peer group disapproval, Dr. Gubbard probably should not embark on further advertising at this time. However, this is only intended as a peg on which to hang discussions of broader issues.

ISSUES FOR DISCUSSION

What information sources tend to be used in the selection of a dentist? (Word-of-mouth recommendation usually comes high on the list, which raises a question about the value of advertising.)

Are there any media that dentists should or should not use for advertising? Specifically, what are students' feelings about direct mail, billboards, and ads on shopping carts?

Are special offers (e.g., two X-rays for $1.00) a suitable way to promote a dental practice?

What kind of image is projected (a) for the dentist, and (b) for the profession generally by ads claiming that a practice caters to cowards?

What are the likely reasons why some dentists advertise and some do not?

TEACHING HINTS

Students tend to have strong views on the issues raised in this case. In the author's experience, although they are in favor of advertising by the professions in principle, they often reveal personal and irrational prejudices about the kind of ads that some dentists use. Reference to the local Yellow Pages should provide the instructor with a varied assortment to stimulate classroom discussion. Analogies can be drawn with advertising by lawyers. (Students tend to categorize those who advertise on television as "ambulance-chasers.") Again in the author's experience, students tend to regard members of the professions who advertise as having to do so because they are less successful. A useful approach can be for the instructor to identify the differences that are important in the advertising of products and services, and then to draw out distinctions between different types of service. For example, why is it considered acceptable to advertise a travel agency or insurance agency, but perhaps not a dental practice?

CASE 10

Traffic Sign Vandalism in Iowa

KATHERINE TOLAND FRITH

INTRODUCTION

In this case students are asked to use research data to develop a theme for a campaign to reduce traffic sign vandalism in Iowa and to recommend a suitable procedure for pretesting. The instructor may also wish to have students create the campaign, although this is not a necessary part of the case. Discussion can be broadened to include consideration of PSAs as part of advertising's contribution to society.

BACKGROUND

Traffic sign vandalism is an increasing problem. A 1983 survey estimated the cost to state departments of transportation of replacing vandalized signs at $50 million, and the costs incurred from resulting injury and tort liability at about the same figure. The signs are a status room decoration for teenagers, especially boys, who engage in vandalism as a group activity.

Vandalizing a highway sign is a crime in Iowa, but few vandals are ever apprehended. The cost to Iowa taxpayers is over $1 million a year. The Iowa Department of Transportation (DOT) has no budget for antivandalism advertising, so plans to mount a publc service campaign. The department hopes this will raise awareness of the serious results of sign vandalism and reduce its incidence in the longer term.

Research is undertaken among Iowa teenagers to help in planning strategy. Survey results showed:

- Widespread involvement in and knowledge of sign vandalism

34

- Ninety-seven percent awareness of the serious results that vandalism could cause

- General lack of awareness of the cost of vandalism to the state and of the penalties involved

Focus group research showed sign vandalism to be regarded as a prank rather than a serious crime, and to have no social stigma attached.

PROBLEM STATEMENT

Iowa DOT has to define objectives for the campaign, generate an appropriate theme and creative treatment, and set up a suitable pretesting procedure.

Constraints

The pretest must be conducted using the *Iowa State Daily*.

Decision Options

Because this case involves the development of a campaign rather than a choice between a defined set of alternatives, this note now concentrates on presenting an account of the actual objectives, campaign theme, and pretesting procedure that were developed.

A random sample of 250 undergraduates were contacted by telephone before and after the advertisements appeared in the *Iowa State Daily*. Different names were selected for the pre and posttest. The advertisements ran a total of eight times over a six week period. The results of the tests are presented in Exhibits 10.1 through 10.4.

Exhibit 10.1

A pre and posttest comparison of students'
knowledge of the fine for stealing signs

	Correct response ($1,000)	Incorrect responses ($25; $100; Other)
Pretest	16%	84%
Posttest	51%	49%

Exhibit 10.2

A pre and posttest comparison of students' knowledge
of the fine for possession of a stolen sign

	Correct response ($100)	Incorrect responses ($25; $1,000; Other)
Pretest	48%	52%
Posttest	57%	43%

Exhibit 10.3

A pre and posttest comparison of students' knowledge
of the jail terms for sign vandalism

	Correct response (30 days)	Incorrect responses (None; 1 year; Other)
Prestest	39%	61%
Posttest	66%	34%

Exhibit 10.4

A pre and posttest comparison of students' knowledge
of the yearly costs to the state of Iowa
for sign vandalism

	Correct response ($1,000,000)	Incorrect responses ($1,000; $500,000; Other)
Pretest	19%	81%
Posttest	22%	78%

CONCLUSIONS AND DISCUSSION

Sign vandalism is a dangerous and costly problem which requires a concerted effort at the national, state, and local level. Yearly national costs for replacing stolen and vandalized signs has been estimated to be in excess of 50 million dollars.

This study suggests that public service advertising can be an effective method for increasing awareness among teenagers of the serious consequences for vandalizing highway signs. In three out of four cases, the knowledge levels of teenagers significantly increased with exposure to the print advertisements. Whether or not the increased knowledge of the fines and penalties for sign vandalism will ultimately effect behavior change is beyond the scope of this study. However, behavior change is the long-term goal of any social-change public-service advertising campaign.

In 1983, Chadda and Carter noted that the state of Wisconsin was able to reduce the incidence of sign vandalism by 57 percent with the use of brochures, media announcements, and educational materials developed for driver's education classes. It is the author's contention that public service advertising combined with other educational materials can be an effective method for reducing sign vandalism throughout the United States.

QUESTIONS
Guiding Questions

What changes in attitude and/or behavior would have to be effected in order to reduce the incidence of traffic sign vandalism?

What kind of themes and appeals could be effective in achieving this?

What objectives might Iowa DOT set for its antivandalism campaign?

Why do you think the *Iowa State Daily* was chosen for the pretest?

What would be a suitable procedure for the pretest to follow?

Discussion Questions

What do advertisers hope to learn from pretesting advertisements?

Assuming no constraints, what would be the most effective media for reaching Iowa teenagers?

How valuable is advertising's contribution to society through PSAs?

REFERENCES

Chadda, Himmat S. and Carter, Everett C. "Sign Vandalism: A Costly and Dangerous National Problem." An unpublished paper submitted for presentation at the 62nd Annual Meeting of the Transportation Research Board. Washington, D.C., January, 1983.

United States Department of Justice, *Sourcebook of Criminal Justice Statistics—1982*. Washington, D.C: Bureau of Justice Statistics, 1983.

CASE 11

Riversedge Marketing, Inc.

TERENCE NEVETT

Most of the cases in this book put students in the position of a manager facing a decision. Riversedge Marketing does not do this. Instead it presents a set of arguments advocating the use of miscellaneous and non-standard media. This note is therefore presented in a different format.

The object of the case is to stimulate students to evaluate the implications of Betsy Gerkman's arguments. How the instructor approaches it will depend on the level of the class and the detail in which students have studied advertising media.

In essence, what Gerkman is suggesting is not that unusual for small clients. The advantage, as she rightly argues, is that small advertisers are isolated not only from bigger-spending competitors, but also from mass consumer campaigns generally. The question then becomes one of whether to be where your heavy users are, or where your competitors are not.

Targeting heavy users may place small advertisers in a situation where their share of voice is so insignificant that their ads cannot make any kind of impression. However, there are some major problems with Gerkman's approach. First, it takes no account of the advertiser's target audience or campaign objectives (though admittedly, this type of client may not have them clearly defined). Second, it offers little possibility for measurement for media planning or campaign evaluation. (It can be argued that for small-budget advertisers measurement is even more important than for their larger counterparts since they have a smaller margin of error.) Third, it can lead to fragmentation; resources are divided among a number of minor media, none of which is capable of sufficient impact.

QUESTIONS
Guiding Questions

What might be other reasonable media options for the small advertiser?

How could an advertiser following Betsy Gerkman's approach evaluate the success of a campaign?

Are there any specific media suggested by Gerkman that you feel are either effective or ineffective?

How far can Gerkman's suggestions be reconciled with the need to define the target audience and set campaign objectives?

Discussion Questions

What kinds of advertisers in your community use the types of media suggested by Gerkman?

You are a small advertiser and Betsy Gerkman is pitching for your business. Part of her pitch includes a recommendation to use the media described in the case. How do you respond?

TEACHING SUGGESTION

The case only gives one side of the story. Students may find it easier to evaluate Gerkman's arguments if they have a basis for comparison. Reference to major media in the area should provide examples of small-budget advertisers following a rather different approach. There are possibilities for role-play, having Gerkman presenting her ideas to a skeptical prospective client.

CASE 12

Aspen Skiing Company Ads

TERENCE NEVETT

INRODUCTION: SUGGESTED TEACHING APPROACH

Rather than confronting students with a decision to be made, Aspen Skiing chronicles an evolving situation in which a famous agency (Hal Riney and Partners) noted for its creativity is hired to develop an image campaign for a ski resort. Accordingly, instead of considering the case as a whole, it is recommended that the instructor takes it in a series of stages, and asks students to analyze the actions of the parties involved at each stage. This note is therefore presented in that way, with questions of more general relevance being included at the end.

BACKGROUND

Aspen is a well-established resort offering excellent skiing in winter and a variety of entertainments and activities in summer. The Aspen Skiing Company operates ski areas on three of the resort's four ski mountains. Advertising for the company is the responsibility of vice-president Bill Turnage and is handled by Denver agency Karsh and Hagan. The account bills $300,000.

STAGE I

Karsh and Hagan's creative approach targets skiers directly. Turnage believes the advertising should stress image differentiation and should concentrate on aspects other than skiing since Aspen is already well known as a ski resort. Turnage therefore sets out to hire Hal Riney and Partners, one of the country's top creative shops. Riney appears to have been somewhat reluctant, but Turnage presses him, even to the extent of raising more money from local business groups. Riney agrees to take the account.

Questions

Turnage is going for the best, but Aspen will be among the agency's smaller clients. What are the pros and cons of being a small client in a large agency?

Should Turnage have persisted in his approach if Riney was indeed unenthusiastic?

Why do agencies have minimum billing requirements? Do these work for or against the interests of clients?

STAGE II

Riney defines Aspen's problems as:

- Negative perceptions including high cost

- Difficult access

- The perception that local people were hostile to outsiders

He proposes a positioning strategy that would distance Aspen from other resorts by avoiding visual clichés associated with skiing. His campaign emphasizes the natural beauty and attractions of Aspen, taking for granted knowledge of the ski facilities. He also coins a new name, "The Aspens," to take in all three ski areas. The campaign is quite different visually from previous resort advertising and uses upmarket magazines backed by radio.

Questions

Comment on this creative approach to resort advertising.

What are the arguments for and against inroducing a new name for the resorts?

What do you consider were the reaons for Riney's choice of media?

STAGE III

The print ads, created with the agency's characteristic elegance, win industry acclaim, but people in Aspen are far less enthusiastic. They criticize the lack of visual reference to skiing and the fact that the 800 number is too small, and complain that the campaign panders to the rich.

The 1988–89 ski season is the best in Aspen's history. Riney follows up with a campaign in similar style for summer. Business is disappointing, though only slightly below the previous year's level.

Questions

Consider the validity of these criticisms.

What, if anything, should Turnage and/or Riney have done in response?

STAGE IV

The 1989–90 ski season brings two major environmental problems:

- Poor snow conditions
- Fierce local debate over a proposal to ban fur sales

Aspen's ski visits are down almost 12 percent, and other ski areas in that part of the state are also affected. Locals are upset because business in Vail is up, but Vail has above-average snowfall, as well as a $6 million media budget. Aspen Highlands also sees a slight increase, but here snow conditions are somewhat better, and a new season pass has probably attracted bargain hunters. The local resort association has to borrow to meet its share of the advertising costs. Members criticize Riney for concentrating on an affluent audience, and some want to refuse to pay.

Questions

To what extent could the Riney advertising be blamed for the drop in business at the Aspens during the winter season 1989–90?

How might the Riney agency have responded to the criticisms of the resort association?

Are there any lessons here for the management of cooperative advertising campaigns?

STAGE V

After research shows that 99 percent of visitors come to the Aspens for skiing, the emphasis in the 1990–91 campaign is on skiing and affordability. Ads show old-style ski equipment and talk about the continuation of the tradition. The resort association accepts the campaign, but it is criticized by local residents who do not understand it.

Questions

What influence should local opinion have on the appearance and content of an advertising campaign for the Aspens?

How relevant is the failure of some local residents to understand the Riney ads?

What are the pros and cons of the indirect, more subtle approach used by Hal Riney compared with a more direct approach to communicating benefits and selling points?

STAGE VI

Katherine A. Boone has taken over as marketing vice-president. Requests for information are running at three times the normal rate.

Questions

What are the tasks facing Katherine Boone?

What changes, if any, should she consider making to (a) the management of advertising for the Aspens, and (b) the creative approach employed by Hal Riney and Partners?

GENERAL DISCUSSION QUESTIONS

Discuss the pros and cons of using sales as a measure of advertising effectiveness in the case of the Aspens.

From an agency viewpoint, what are the problems that arise when handling a cooperative campaign, especially when it is financed by organizations representing a range of different viewpoints and interests?

Should an advertising campaign for a ski resort be approached differently from a campaign for a supermarket product?

CASE 13

Canyon Breweries: Gloster Beer*

Roxanne Hovland

INTRODUCTION

The focus of this case is the advertising of "nonalcoholic" beer that, despite its name, does contain a small amount of alcohol. The question is whether the advertising, because of the information included (or excluded) or the images projected, unfairly places alcoholics at risk. No special knowledge is required of students.

BACKGROUND/OVERVIEW

A research analyst recognizes a possible ethical dilemma which could create tension between the analyst and his superiors and/or between the agency and the client. Since the product involved is relatively new, and there are no legal or other guidelines for its advertising, the seriousness of the potential problem raised is not known. (No one knows for sure how many recovering alcoholics have relapsed as a result of nonalcoholic beer.) The analyst also doesn't know whether anyone else considers this a potentially serious problem.

PROBLEM STATEMENT

Students should first develop several alternative actions that the analyst could take. One of the first issues to address is whether Chris Potter should even voice his concerns about the proposed campaign.

Constraints

One constraint is financial. Significantly altering the campaign could double the expense which, presumably, would have to be covered by the agency. There would also be twice as much time devoted to this campaign. The analyst is constrained by his own professional ambition. Whatever action he takes, he runs the risk of alienating someone in a way that could affect his career. Though there are no specific legal constraints (other than the usual rules regarding deception), public sentiment toward the advertiser and the brand is always a consideration.

Decision Options

1. Chris could ask to be relieved of the assignment. He would avoid having to make a decision, but his supervisor might not look too favorably on this. And, if he truly does think something should be changed in the advertising, he loses any opportunity to get it changed.

2. He could recommend using the campaign as it is. This would be the fastest, cheapest alternative for everyone, at least in the short run. However, Chris has to ignore his concerns, which ultimately may prove valid. He'd feel pretty bad if the client received a lot of complaints due to the ads.

3. Chris could recommend revising the campaign so the alcohol content is displayed more prominently in both the print and broadcast ads. This might serve as a warning to someone who shouldn't consume even a small amount of alcohol. This would incur some additional cost, but it would be less than if the entire campaign were scrapped.

4. Chris could go a step further and recommend the addition of a warning that would alert people as to the potential risk associated with this amount of alcohol. A recovering alcoholic wouldn't need to call a counselor, but would know not to drink this beverage just by seeing the warning. This could further increase the cost of producing the campaign, and it also might create unnecessary anxiety about the product among nonalcoholics.

PREFERRED DECISION

A good compromise solution is for Chris to recommend displaying the alcohol content more prominently in print and on the label and including it in the broadcast commercials. This gives all consumers important information which they can use accordingly. This might serve as a sufficient signal to someone for whom a small amount of alcohol is dangerous. Given adequate, accurate information, the consumer can safely take responsibility. This does not alleviate the problem of the advertising's imagery creating a psychological trigger that might prompt a relapse. But, in reality, these images are everywhere, not just in advertising. Alcoholics successfully cope with many psychological triggers every day.

QUESTIONS

Guiding Questions

Is there anything illegal about the ad campaign as it has been described?

Is there anything deceptive about the campaign?

Are there enough alcoholics in this country for this to be a significant group in the population?

Are there other kinds of products where there have been similar problems associated with the advertising?

To whom or to what should Chris owe his loyalty in this situation?

Discussion Questions

Is this particular audience (recovering alcoholics) so vulnerable that one can't assume them to be capable of taking responsibility for themselves?

Have Chris's feelings about his friends impaired his normally good instincts?

Is there something inherently deceptive about calling a beverage "nonalcoholic" when it still has some alcohol in it?

Do the positive attributes of this product outweigh its potential danger to certain consumers?

Is there anything about this situation that should cause Chris to abandon his usual policy of complete honesty?

Jacobs Laboratories Task Force*

TERENCE NEVETT

INTRODUCTION

In this case students are asked to consider the pros and cons of using a celebrity spokesperson to endorse a product targeted at the mature market, as well as some of the more general issues related to celebrity endorsements. There is also a political dimension in terms of Palmateer's relations with her superior.

BACKGROUND

Marian Palmateer is advertising manager of Jacobs Laboratories, an organization marketing consumer and prescription products nationwide. Sales of Jacobs' consumer products, which acccount for 60 percent of total revenue, have been growing at a slower rate over the period 1987–89 than those of prescription products. A task force set up by the company's president recommends targeting health-conscious consumers 65+ with a premium-priced multivitamin tablet. This recommendation is accepted, and Palmateer sets the agency to work on the launch campaign.

The agency proposes the use of a celebrity spokesperson. When Palmateer seeks approval of this idea from Eric Spencer, marketing v.p., he is very doubtful and warns Palmateer that she will be held personally accountable if things go wrong.

PROBLEM STATEMENT

Should Palmateer proceed with the campaign? (This involves consideration of the suitability of a celebrity spokesperson and also of how Palmateer should confront the political situation within the company.)

Constraints

- Jacobs has limited corporate experience in marketing consumer products, and none in marketing to the mature market.

- The client and agency personnel involved are all relatively young.

- Spencer's background is in pharmaceutical rather than consumer products.

- Spencer does not accept the celebrity concept, and is unlikely to fight for it within the company.

- The vitamin market is highly fragmented, and is dominated by private brands.

- The advertising budget is based on the anticipated market share in the first year.

Decision Options

Palmateer is basically in a go – no go situation. Her decision should take into account both the pros and cons of using a celebrity, and her position within the company if she decides to go ahead.

Use of Celebrity

Pros:

- Visibility in a competitive and fragmented market

- Assistance in establishing the credibility of Jacobs and Product Z (Spencer thinks Jacobs should have no worries here, but he is referring to the pharmaceutical trade, not consumers.)

- Emphasis of selling points by spokesperson (This is of limited value to Jacobs because Z is a parity product.)

- Portrayal of spokesperson as the "benefit"

- Consumer identification with a properly selected spokesperson

Cons:

- The cost of a suitable celebrity could seriously damage media effectiveness by taking some $500,000 of the $3 million available.

- Effectiveness could be reduced by public cynicism about the use of celebrities.

- Problems might arise during the campaign, including the death of the person being featured.

- Consumers might remember the celebrity but not the product.

- The use of a celebrity endorser seems likely to involve Palmateer in a political struggle within the company.

Political Situation

Spencer's parting remark shows Palmateer to be in an exposed position, and thus an obvious scapegoat if things go wrong. This could include not only aspects of the creative execution, but also perhaps blame for the failure of Product Z to reach its target share of the market. (Nothing is said in the case about how the advertising is to be evaluated.) Whatever form the campaign eventually takes, Palmateer could protect her position by having a final presentation to Hannigan, Spencer, and other members of top management. If they approve the campaign, then Palmateer cannot be held solely responsible for the outcome.

PREFERRED OPTION

There is no clear choice here. The concept of using a highly visible celebrity to break into a congested market has much to recommend it, but probably not at the expense of taking one-sixth of the company's media allocation. Given that Z is a parity product, it is unlikely to have any major benefits that could form the basis of a presenter-style commercial. This would seem to detract from the usefulness of a straightforward endorsement. If the intention is to demonstrate an active lifestyle with which mature consumers can identify, which Palmateer gives as one of the reasons, the use of a famous face might even distract the audience's attention from the main message.

Spencer's point about the risks involved is also valid. Serious illness, disability, or death might well be perceived as reflecting unfavorably on the product. Such an eventuality would also mean that Jacobs would have to write off their investment in the person concerned and prepare a new campaign. This is a risk they probably cannot afford to take.

Students might therefore consider what alternative approaches the agency could offer. For example, if the objective is to demonstrate a healthy lifestyle, is there any need for the people portrayed to be recognizable by consumers?

QUESTIONS
Guiding Questions

How should Palmateer respond to Spencer?

Could Palmateer justify spending $500,000 on a celebrity endorser?

Discussion Questions

What are the characteristics of a good presenter?

What issues would arise if Jacobs were to consider using a presenter from another age group—for example, an active person under thirty?

Which celebrity presenters do students consider are effective/ineffective celebrity spokespersons in current TV commercials? (Note: According to researcher Dave Vadehra, consumer polls over an eight-year period have consistently shown Bill Cosby to be the most convincing and believable celebrity endorser.)

REFERENCES

There is a useful summary of the issues involved in the use of celebrity endorsers in Rossiter and Percy's *Advertising and Promotion Management* (McGraw – Hill, 1987). For some of the problems that confront advertisers see Howard Schlossberg, "Allure of Celebrity Endorsers Starts to Fade," *Marketing News* (June 11, 1990), 6–7; Mindy Weinstein and Scott Donaton, "Celebs' Star Sinking in Ads," *Advertising Age* (August 28, 1989), 48; "Dead Stars are In," *Advertising Age* (August 14, 1989), 44.

CASE 15

SharpVision Optical Company*

SEVGIN EROGLÜ

INTRODUCTION

The main objectives of this case are twofold: a) to show the importance of proper research methodology in terms of providing useful and meaningful information for management, and b) to give students a chance to evaluate a consumer research project and to interpret its results in order to recommend specific strategies.

BACKGROUND

SharpVision Optical is a company which has been experiencing market share losses in the last two years due to increasing competition from the new entrants into its traditionally non-competitive market area. The company's typically traditional top management has only recently created a research department in the organization and has hired Jenny Dorsh as promotions and research director to head it. In order to understand consumers' expectations about optical stores, as well as their opinions about SharpVision and its competition, Jenny Dorsh and her staff conducted a regional consumer research project. In the information received, SharpVision now has some insights about what marketing and advertising strategies to pursue.

PROBLEM STATEMENT

The students are first asked to evaluate the research methodology used in the case with particular attention to statement of objectives and sampling strategy. Then, the next step is to try to make sense out of the collected information, i.e., interpretation of the data given in the text and tables. Finally, the students are asked to suggest strategies for SharpVision in the light of the data and its interpretation.

Constraints

The major constraint that is deliberately imposed on the case analyzed here is limited information. With the exception of competition, students are given no information on budgetary or other constraints, or on resources. The intention here is to force them to focus solely on the research and obtained data without broadening the scope of the problem.

FOCAL TOPICS
Evaluation of the Research Design

The research is complete in that focus groups were conducted prior to questionnaire design, the survey instrument was pre-tested, and data was collected, edited, coded, and analyzed properly. At this point it is instructive and useful to talk about advantages (e.g., helpful to determine the scale items) and disadvantages (e.g., difficult to get a representative sample, moderator might bias results) of focus groups. The instructor can also create some discussion on the pros and cons of the telephone survey used in the case and compare and contrast it with mail and personal interview techniques.

The most important limitation of the research design is its sampling strategy. Although the sample size of 400 is acceptable for a study of this nature (it is, in fact, the rule-of-thumb sample size), its composition leaves much to be desired. Seventy-five percent of the sample, for example, comes from the current customers of SharpVision. As much as this group's opinions are critical, it is even more important to understand awareness and attitudes of non-customers for SharpVision. Furthermore, examination of the respondent profile data (Exhibit 15.1) indicates a heavy bias toward low education, low income, blue collar, female, and young population. Given that three-quarters of the sample are current customers, this profile might represent the characteristics of the typical SharpVision customer base. On the other hand, since simple random sampling technique was used, as opposed to a more accurate sampling method (such as stratified random sampling) which would select from the population on a more proportionate basis, we are not sure if this sample is truly representative of the entire customer base of SharpVision. The instructor could take this opportunity to review, for example, differences between random and non-random sampling techniques, and how they might affect research accuracy.

Interpretation of Survey Data

The data given in the body of the text does not need much interpretation, so it is more useful to concentrate on the tables. It is fairly clear from Exhibit 15.2 that while SharpVision is perceived to be superior on the convenience dimension (both hours and store locations), it is not considered to have helpful salespeople, a finding which is likely to surprise top management which has traditionally assumed their employees to be the company's greatest asset. A finding that, in a way, supports this perception of employees is the low rating on timely service. Surprisingly, perceptions about SharpVision in the context of prices are very favorable, another finding that is likely to surprise top management.

There seems to be a significant difference between female and male respondents in terms of favorability toward SharpVision (Exhibit 15.3). Although this is an important finding, students should keep in mind the very small sample of male respondents that were surveyed (Exhibit 15.1). The possibility that this particular information can be an artifact of the sampling bias should at least be mentioned during the case discussion.

Finally, the students should easily see from Exhibit 15.4 the major sources that helped consumers to be aware of SharpVision.

Marketing Recommendations Based on the Data

This case is more suited to a discussion of the research process than strategy formulation. However, based on the research findings, the students should be able to suggest some marketing and advertising recommendations. For example, based on the data about what attributes consumers value in selecting an optical store, and how SharpVision rates on these attributes, students could speculate on what appeals and message types to use to accentuate the existing strengths and minimize the weaknesses of the company. In a similar vein, students can talk about various media alternatives by drawing both on the case material and their own experiences. The marketing and advertising strategies of optical stores in students' local area could help shed some light on what actions are to be recommended for SharpVision. The instructor may also want to have the class design and/or administer a short questionnaire to compare the images of two or three prominent local optical stores.

GUIDING QUESTIONS

1. Evaluate the project in terms of proper research methodology for the problem at hand, making any suggestions that would improve its worth.

Pay particular attention to appropriateness of research objectives and sampling issues.

2. What specific conclusions can be reached from the evaluation of the survey findings?

3. What specific marketing and advertising strategy recommendations should Jenny Dorsh make to the top management on the basis of these findings?

CASE 16

Rachman's Discount Store*

ROGER DICKINSON

Editor's note: Professor Dickinson is a leading retailing scholar and a former department store executive. He demonstrates in this analysis that the principles set out in advertising textbooks are generally manufacturer-oriented, and do not necessarily have the same validity in other areas of business.

INTRODUCTION

Executives frequently have to make decisions with little relevant information, at least of the kind desired. The budgeting of money for advertising for the company is an example of that. Executives know that nearly all successful retailers do advertise. They also know that they can only accurately measure part of the short-term impact of the advertising. The residual of the short-term and the long-term impacts cannot be measured. Further, the long-term impact itself can be quite large. Literature estimates that I have seen range up to 70 percent. In the May – June 1990 *Harvard Business Review*, p. 53, Abraham and Lodish in a supplier context offer at least 50 percent as the long-term impact.

BACKGROUND/OVERVIEW

All of the proposals of academics on specific procedures for the budgeting of advertising money for the total firm are defective in some way. The focus for many years was straight marginal analysis, derived from Alfred Marshall and later Joel Dean (*Managerial Economics*, 1951, Prentice-Hall). Continue to advertise so long as the benefits exceed the costs. While philosophically of value, as a practical tool this is obviously not useful for most firms (non-mail order) for the reasons specified in the above introduction.

A favored procedure of academics is the objective and task. The objective and task basically suggests that the executive establish objectives (usually communication objectives; see Colley, 1961, *Defining Advertising Goals for Measured Advertising Results*, Association of National Advertisers) and then, as a final step, relate these objectives to profitability. Recognize that the final step has all the limitations of marginal analysis. And if you can calculate the benefits for one set of advertising alternatives, why not for all? However, recognize that hopefully all retail executives will establish their advertising objectives before advertising, simply as a part of reasonably intelligent decision making. Know where you want to get.

We also know that retail firms will in general react to changes in the marketing mix (including money spent on advertising) of important competition. If the most important competitor doubles the amount spent on advertising, most effective retailers will react. Retailers may also see bad economic times as a chance to grab market share. Thus they may increase advertising while they think competitors are asleep.

PROBLEM STATEMENT

The problem is to devise a method of establishing the money allocated to advertising for the total company (i.e., not among departments or among the months of the year). In general, the more systematic and databased the decision, the better off the decision maker will be. However, garbage-in by any perspective generates garbage-out.

Constraints

The prime constraint in establishing the dollar value of advertising is that the company should have the "money" to pay for it. Indeed, the literature has seen this as a budgeting technique, "the all you can afford approach." And in some conditions this makes eminent sense. For example, if that segment of short-term contribution that is readily calculable exceeds the out-of-pocket cost for the advertising (and one assumes that the short-term and the long-term implications are at least collectively positive), then the executive should continue advertising until diminishing returns bring the returns under the cost. A very important point with respect to advertising budgeting is made by understanding this point. The actions of companies make it very clear that most are not in the position where short-term benefits are greater than the out-of-pocket costs. Other short-term benefits and long-term benefits are needed to justify advertising dollars.

Decision Options

The choice of method will likely be from among the options suggested above, plus some others we will indicate in the preferred decision section. Every "principles" of advertising or marketing text lists options for how to budget advertising.

PREFERRED DECISION

As many retail texts tell us, most retailers budget by the percentage of sales—past, present or future. Perhaps the most important aspect for the professor to grasp is that contrary to what many economists suggest, this need not imply that sales cause advertising. For many executives this is benchmarking. See what the most effective companies similar to you (in areas such as size, competitive milieux, type, stage of development) do or have done; and then imitate, considering the factors seen as different, e.g., what specific competitors are doing. The easiest way to "standardize" benchmarking is by some percentage of sales. Recognize further that the percentage of sales is directly tied to the operating statement and will react quickly to changes in the economic environment for most firms.

Recognize that the results of advertising should be calculated (estimated) after each advertisement (or campaign) and integrated into the information system to aid with future advertising. Also recognize that the above method should be used in conjunction with communication or other objectives. The percentage of sales only establishes the dollar value. Establishing objectives should be part of any decision to which important allocation of money is relevant.

QUESTIONS

Ask any student who would like to use a technique such as the objective and task (that they were probably "taught" in principles) to go through each step, arriving at a budget.

REFERENCE

Dickinson, Roger, Myron Gable, and Tom Smith (1991), "Percentage of Sales Method of Advertising Budgeting: A Retail Perspective," *Proceedings of the Academy of Marketing Science/American Collegiate Retailing Association Retailing Conference*, Richmond, VA (complete reference not available at time of going to press).

CASE 17

Carswell's Restaurants*

TERENCE NEVETT

INTRODUCTION

The facts presented here concern an advertising decision that is part of a larger market targeting problem. Advertising cannot reasonably be considered in isolation from the questions of which market segment(s) offer(s) the best prospects for Carswell's, and what changes, if any, are needed in their basic offering.

BACKGROUND

Carswell's is a family-owned chain of some 50 restaurants concentrated in Florida and Georgia. Sales for 1990 totaled $21 million. The chain offers reasonably-priced family dining with friendly service.

Carswell's spend $725,000 on advertising, concentrating on areas where restaurants are situated. They use a mix of TV and radio for image reinforcement, and newspapers for promotions, especially coupons. The copyline, "The Place You Love to Eat," has been unchanged for nearly 20 years.

After three decades of growth, sales remained static in 1989 and 1990. Owner Jim Carswell thinks advertising may bear some of the responsibility and calls a meeting with two of his top executives. This turns into a wide-ranging discussion of the chain's future.

PROBLEM STATEMENT

In the case, Carswell identifies two problems:

- If the advertising has worked in the past, why is it not working now?

58

• If it is not working, what action should Carswell's take?

However, students should consider whether, in fact, there is a more fundamental problem facing Carswell's, and if so, is it one to which advertising can provide an answer?

Constraints

• The conservative orientation of the company and its owner—belief in traditional values, advertising unchanged for 20 years, etc.—is unlikely to change.

• Carswell's are unlikely to increase their advertising expenditure per customer, which is already running at almost twice the national rate.

Decision Options

These are represented by the opposing viewpoints presented at the meeting.

Di Luca argues that Carswell's advertising has not responded to demographic changes. It is still targeted at traditional two-parent families who probably will only represent 50 percent of the population by the year 2000. The firm has done nothing to target seniors in Florida, baby boomers in cities like Atlanta, or ethnic groups. The way for the business to grow is to expand the customer base.

Zorn argues that Carswell's is a modest-sized company with a modest advertising budget. To make an impact they have to concentrate on one segment; otherwise the advertising appeal will have to be too generalized, and the media effort too fragmented. Targeting a new segment might also alienate the existing customer base. Carswell's should therefore retain their basic family appeal, but widen it to include more emphasis on children.

Carswell believes the basic message that has worked so well in the past is even more relevant today, since it represents a core value in American society. He also thinks they should continue to stress service.

In order to exploit the segments di Luca has identified, Carswell's would need to be considerably reorganized, tailoring different offerings to each segment. This would probably involve creating several new identities for groups of restaurants within the chain, and these would have to be promoted separately, so losing the synergy obtained through coordination of the company image and of promotional materials. Expenditure would be fragmented, which would lessen its effectiveness. The existing customer base would probably also be alienated.

Even though service is important and is rated highly by customers, it tends to be weak as an advertising claim, not least because it is so difficult to demonstrate. Carswell's also have only inferential evidence about their standard of service. Given the number of customers nationally who are dissatisfied but don't complain, Carswell's have no room for complacency.

The shift in emphasis to children would be more in line with Carswell's historic strategy, and the family appeal could also presumably be broadened to include seniors. Modifications to the basic theme would have to be handled carefully so that Carswell's did not find themselves competing for children's patronage against Ronald MacDonald.

PREFERRED DECISION

Jim Carswell's instinct over the years has been not to change what he sees as a winning game plan, and it is usually poor policy in any business to make drastic changes without good cause. Carswell's are not in real trouble and are not losing ground. On the other hand, the dangers of alienating existing loyal customers are considerable. The segments identified by di Luca have potential, but Carswell's cannot be all things to all people. It is recommended that they preserve their family image, but modify it gradually so as to appeal specifically to children and seniors. Jim Carswell may be right about the ads providing reassurance in a troubled time.

QUESTIONS
Guiding Questions

What is the role of advertising in selecting a place to eat?

Is it possible for a single type of restaurant and a single advertising appeal to cover more than one of the segments identified by di Luca?

What are the problems faced in trying to show good service visually in an ad?

Is an increased appeal to children likely to alienate some of Carswell's adult customers?

Discussion Questions

What is the value of coupons is advertising a restaurant?

Should restaurants encourage customers to complain?

TEACHING SUGGESTIONS

It is easy to have students relate to some aspects of this case by involving their experiences of places where they have eaten, and sometimes where they have worked. It is also useful to introduce examples of current restaurant advertising in the local area. (Schools in the area served by Bob Evans restaurants may find that chain's advertising provides an interesting comparison.)

The viewpoints of the three characters in the meeting lend themselves to role play.

CASE 18

Sunburst Orange Juice, Florida*

PEGGY J. KRESHEL AND JILL D. SWENSON

INTRODUCTION

At the most basic level, this case deals with defining target audiences and evaluating creative executions designed to address those audiences. At a minimum, students will become aware of the limitations of relying solely upon demographic descriptions.

More importantly, the objective of this case is to heighten student consciousness regarding gender roles and their portrayal in advertising executions. In short, it is a case about the power of stereotypes, both subtle and dramatic, in advertising.

Students are expected to be familiar with using syndicated data, such as MRI and SMRB, to develop demographic profiles of product users. No prior knowledge of the sociology of family and gender is required; sufficient information is provided in the case.

BACKGROUND

Sunburst, a ready-to-drink orange juice, has been very successful with a simple, straight-forward creative strategy: "Sunburst, a part of every family's breakfast." Creative executions have focused upon images of the "traditional" American family at breakfast and have met with strong client approval.

As suggested by discussion in the case, the orange-juice-for-breakfast strategy remains sound and is the basis of the creative execution concept which the students are asked to evaluate. That execution, like those in the past, draws largely upon stereotypical images of domestic life (e.g., home, family, parental roles, breakfast, etc.).

In addition to syndicated data, students are provided with information on "The American Family." This information suggests that demographic and sociological structures of "family" in the United States are substantially different from those in the creative execution; households are becoming smaller and increasingly diverse.

PROBLEM STATEMENT

Should Maria Martinez accept the proposed concept?

Decision Options

The case draws attention to the importance of consumer identification with advertising portrayals. Students are then asked to evaluate the proposed creative concept. They have two decision options. If they believe the portrayals in the execution are inappropriate (e.g., outmoded, stereotypical, offensive, etc.), Martinez should direct the creative team to try again. In this instance, the instructor might ask students to offer two executional ideas to get the creative team started. Alternatively, Martinez can accept the executional concept, in which case students can be asked to develop a pitch to sell the working concept to the client. In either instance, of course, students should be asked to justify their decision.

PREFERRED DECISION

Despite the fact that the portrayals in the proposed execution are, indeed, stereotypical, given the objective of this case, there is no "preferred" decision. The very fact that students' attention is drawn to the issue of stereotypical portrayals should increase students' awareness of the use of stereotypes, stimulate critical thinking about the use of stereotypes in advertising, and lead to animated classroom discussion. The instructor most likely will choose to evaluate the student on the basis of evidence of critical thinking with regard to the choice of either option.

In addition to the obvious kinds of management questions which may be posed, several additional questions are suggested below. These questions can be used to guide students through the case and to focus their attention/ discussion on the specific issues of stereotypical portrayals in advertising raised by the case.

QUESTIONS
Guiding Questions

1. What is a family?
   (Probe here for recognition of "non-traditional" household types such

as single-parent, two opposite-sex singles, two same-sex singles, one-person households, etc.)

2. How has family life in America changed in the last decade?
   (Probe for changes in occupational roles and domestic responsibilities in addition to those sociological changes suggested in answering question one; e.g., who does the cooking? shopping? Also probe for changes in mealtime rituals.)

3. What is a stereotype?

4. What stereotypes exist in the proposed execution?
   (Probe for gender roles, both of men and women; family; race; class; age; etc. Probe also for stereotypes about what constitutes work, home, and breakfast.)

5 By excluding portrayals of certain kinds of families, do you fail to communicate with part of your target audience?

Discussion Questions

1. What role do stereotypes play in society; in your day-to-day life?

2. What role do stereotypes play in advertising? What function do they serve?

3. How are stereotypes perpetuated? How do new portrayals become stereotypical? Are old stereotypes simply replaced with new ones?
   (It might be useful here to point out that the perpetuation of stereotypes may be subtle and unintentional. For example, advertising researchers conducting content analyses of women's role portrayals frequently classify those portrayals as "traditional" and "non-traditional." One might legitimately ask, at what point will "women in business acting in management roles" no longer be considered "non-traditional?" In this case, is the label used unintentionally perpetuating stereotypical images?)

4. Are stereotypes constructed out of "ideals" (e.g., idealized images of "family")? Demographic averages?

5. Do stereotypes function to maintain the status quo?

6. Does targeting necessarily invoke stereotypes?
   (Recent controversies over brands such as Dakota, Uptown, and Powermaster are sure to stimulate discussion.)

7. Can advertising work without stereotypes? Can we escape stereotypes?

The exercise of critically evaluating the creative alternatives which might be suggested by students who have asked the creative team to start again will quite likely provide an excellent starting point for discussion of many of these questions.

CASE 19

Karlin-Martin Advertising*

TERENCE NEVETT

INTRODUCTION

The subject of agency – client relations receives little attention in advertising textbooks, even though retaining profitable clients is crucial to an agency's success. This case traces the deteriorating relations between a small but growing agency and one of its first clients.

BACKGROUND

Shortly after the Karlin – Martin agency had opened for business, Joe Karlin persuaded David Ginsberg to place the advertising for his two stores through the agency. Karlin – Martin produced work for Ginsberg's that was of a high creative standard.

Though both agency and client were somewhat haphazard in their administration, the relationship did not run into serious problems. This could have been because David Ginsberg did not know what he was entitled to expect from an agency. However, when his wife Ruth took over responsibility for advertising, she was far more demanding—unreasonably so from the agency's point of view. The partners adopted various strategies to avoid spending too much time on the account, which had a low priority within the agency. The result was that Ruth, who already had a low view of advertising people, believed she was being neglected. Eventually relations reached a point where Ruth decided that Ginsberg's would stop advertising for six months on a trial basis to see what effect this had on sales. If there were no effect, then the firm would stop advertising completely.

PROBLEM STATEMENT

Faced with this situation, what action if any should the agency take?

Constraints

- David and Ruth have little knowledge of advertising or its relationship to consumer behavior.

- Karlin and Martin have no interest in or aptitude for administration.

- Ginsberg's is a low priority client, demanding a level of service that is unrealistic given their modest expenditure.

- Ruth is in a powerful position personally, being married to the owner of the business.

- Loss of the Ginsberg account may have an adverse effect on the agency's other clients.

Decision Options

The agency could do nothing. This might be argued from two points of view. First, the relationship might be seen as past saving, so that the agency should waste no further time on Ginsberg's. Second, the agency might believe that Ginsberg's will eventually find they need advertising and will then probably come back to Karlin – Martin.

Alternatively, the agency could try to save the situation and persuade Ruth to change her mind. However, her letter does not read like another attempt to gain attention, and even if some kind of reconciliation were possible, it would probably be a stop-gap measure at best, given the history of her relations with Karlin – Martin. It seems, therefore, that a success-ful outcome would need somehow to involve David Ginsberg to give the agency – client relationship a degree of stability. Martin might justifiably telephone him and ask for a meeting with him and Ruth to try and resolve the situation. He would have to be careful, however, to avoid giving the impression of going over Ruth's head, which would make her even more angry and possibly alienate David too. Ruth is obviously the wrong person to be responsible for advertising, as the last sentence of her letter shows, though it would be difficult to persuade her husband that she would be better employed in some other capacity.

Karlin and Martin would also have to convince Ginsberg's of the need to advertise. Ruth may well be right in saying that the business was growing before they signed with the agency. They were, however, already doing a modest amount of advertising dealing direct with the media, so to stop completely at this time is a drastic step. Ruth's idea of a six-month cessation would show very little because the business would still be benefiting from customers created by advertising. In particular, it is likely that Karlin – Martin's highly creative advertising would have a carryover effect, with prospects making a mental note to look at Ginsberg's next time they were downtown or needed the type of clothing Ginsberg's carries. This source of sales will gradually dry up when advertising stops.

PREFERRED DECISION

There is no way to tell whether Karlin–Martin could save the Ginsberg account if they were to try. Essentially the agency has to decide whether it is worth the time and trouble involved. This means balancing the opportunity to do good work against the excessive degree of attention they will still probably have to give. The prime consideration ought to be whether the account is profitable, but an agency as disorganized as Karlin–Martin probably would not even know this (the real-life Karlin and Martin didn't).

If the agency does decide to try and save the situation, it muct come up with a counterproposal to Ruth's six month spending freeze, which also gives Ginsberg's a better indication of whether their advertising is actually working for them. It would be a simple matter to determine whether a customer was a repeat purchaser, was recommended by a friend, came after seeing an advertisement, or noticed something of interest in the store window. (For example, the customer could be asked to fill out a brief questionnaire while the sales clerk was dealing with the payment.) This approach would not only give Ginsberg's the information they want without the risks involved in stopping advertising; it would also allow Karlin–Martin to demonstrate that they have expertise in areas other than the creation of advertising, which could be of use to Ginsberg's in building their business.

QUESTIONS
Guiding Questions

What would be the advantages to Karlin–Martin of (a) saving and (b) relinquishing the Ginsberg account?

Are there any lessons the agency could learn from the history of its relationship with Ginsberg's?

Are there any steps Karlin–Martin could take, assuming they saved the account, that would effectively "neutralize" Ruth?

Discussion Questions

Does Ruth's idea of a six-month moratorium on advertising make sense from a research point of view?

Could the agency have taken steps at an earlier stage that would have prevented the situation from escalating?

Was Martin's "time-rationing" approach justified?

To what extent is it inevitable that a growing agency will part company with its early clients?

WHAT ACTUALLY HAPPENED

The agency gambled that Ginsberg's would find their sales falling without advertising, and so decided to wait. In fact, sales increased, so Ginsberg's decided to do no further advertising.

Postscript: there were probably several explanations for the increase, including seasonal and general economic factors, and some carryover from the Karlin–Martin advertising. These were apparently unrecognized by Ruth and David. Subsequently, their business began to decline, but they could not bring themselves to accept that the reason might be that they had stopped advertising. Eventually they were obliged to sell out.

TEACHING SUGGESTIONS

Students are generally warned to present facts in an analytical framework rather than sequentially. In this case, however, the facts need to be considered in sequence in order to understand how the breakdown in relations came about. (This may be compared to a medical student watching the progress of an infection.) The instructor may in fact wish to approach the case historically and examine the actions of the principal characters in a series of "snapshots," analyzing their actions and responses at each stage.

The case can be used to open a broader discussion of agency–client relations. The framework suggested by Bovee and Arens of the four Cs— chemistry, communication, conduct, and changes—can be helpful here. In particular, it should be pointed out that there must be a certain inevitability in terms of conflict. Clients that do not grow will continue to need a small agency, and if their agency grows, their respective needs diverge.

CASE 20

Alma Cheese Co., Austria

Ronald A. Fullerton

INTRODUCTION

Travelling from Vienna across Austria by train, a young Austrian marketing executive ponders the results of advertising pretesting done in the United States. She has to report to management the next day. Her firm, the Alma Cheese Co., is a producer of quality cheese which is trying to increase its sales in the U.S. market. Austrian cheese, however, is not well known in the U.S. Moreover, Alma is of modest size and resources compared to much of the competition. Issues in the case include: analyzing creative strategies, appraising advertising research methods and results, evaluating the appropriate role of advertising research, and above all, attempting to make decisions about a faraway market without the aids of costly research and consulting. All of these issues have to be approached from the perspective of an Austrian marketer—a good exercise in understanding international conditions. Hopefully, the case will give students unfamiliar with Central Europe some idea of life and business there.

The young executive and her journey are fictional; the rest is not. The case can be understood by students with widely differing backgrounds. Those who have had exposure to market/advertising research should be able to do the most penetrating technical analyses of the pretest results; those with humanities backgrounds, on the other hand, may do better analyzing the conceptual interplay which closes the case. Students familiar with the advertising business may most readily recognize some of the stock thinking and stereotyping which characterizes it on both sides of the Atlantic. All students should be able to look up current monetary exchange rates and calculate figures given in Austrian schillings into U.S. dollars. In recent years, the exchange rate has ranged between 10 and 14 schillings per dollar.

BACKGROUND/OVERVIEW

The environmental situation is that Austria is not known to Americans (or most others, for that matter) for its cheeses, which currently account for less than six percent of the dollar cost of cheese imports into the United States. The fact that the Austrian cheeses are of acknowledged quality has not made much difference, perhaps because it is not widely known. The Alma Cheese Co. cannot "ride" the reputation of Austrian cheese because in effect there is no reputation. It lacks the budget to buy share of mind through massive barrages of advertising. What Alma needs is a message which will be highly effective when expressed through a few exposures in a quality media vehicle—a message which will convey upon Alma cheese a distinct and appealing quality. Alma's current U.S. advertising themes have been Alpine landscapes and product quality—both of which are, unfortunately, likely to remind Americans of Swiss cheeses.

Americans do have distinct and positive images concerning Austria, according to research done at the Economic University of Vienna. This research further suggests that these images could be linked with Austrian exported products through a conditioning process in advertising—country image transfer. In order to see if such a phenomenon could 1) occur and 2) help Alma, a test of three prototype ads has been carried out in the United States. One of the ads tested follows Alma's traditional pattern. A second emphasizes product quality and people enjoying eating cheese; the people are European, but not necessarily Austrian. The third ad is an attempt to associate the product with well-known and positive images of Austria (the Mozart Boys' Choir in this case). Results of a portfolio test show that the second ad did best.

PROBLEM STATEMENT

The basic problem here is whether Alma should adopt a new message strategy in the U.S. market. Students should recognize this and understand why a change is being considered; they should realize that issues of research, creative strategy, and firm constraints are all in play as the decision maker, Ms. Molke, attempts to prepare her report to management. Students should be familiar with the three creative strategies, including the theoretical rationale underlying the country image transfer strategy, and should be able to interpret systematically the research results presented. They should understand how the pretest was conducted and be able to describe the sample chosen. Close examination of specifics ought to precede and lead to broader discussion of topics such as critiquing advertising research techniques, research versus intuitive judgment in creating advertising, and the formulation of export strategies by small firms.

Constraints

Constraints are important in this case.

There is an explicit *budget constraint* stated early in the case; note that the monetary figure given includes many of Alma's export markets, not just the United States, and that it is far lower when the schillings are converted to dollars. (Any student who blathers thoughtlessly about network TV advertising must be quickly put right.)

A second constraint is management's explicit insistence on high *quality media vehicles*, an U.S. example of which would be *Gourmet* magazine. (An alert student might track down *Gourmet's* current rate card.)

The third constraint in the case is *time*: Ms. Molke has to make her report the next day. It is implied that there will be no more testing or discussion after that, but rather action.

Decision Options

The pretest results give strongest support to the well-done "generic" type of cheese ad. However, one could also argue for "country image transfer" on the following grounds:

- It might show its effectiveness with repetition—assuming some way can be found to achieve sufficient exposures despite the firm's ad budget constraints.

- A better creative execution than that in the test ad (an admitted prototype) could be done. In particular, an image evocative of Austria but closer to food than the Mozart Boys' Choir might be used—for example, elegantly dressed men and women enjoying champagne and cheese at the dinner intermission at the Vienna State Opera House. In the pretest, American respondents explicitly questioned the relevance of the constumed Mozart boys to cheese.

Beyond these options, another would be to combine elements of the "traditional landscape" and the "generic" ads. Still another would be to stick with the present strategy—which is not causing losses—and accept modest growth in the U.S. market. After all, Alma has other export markets, some of which might be easier to cultivate.

PREFERRED DECISION

Judging from the test results, the "generic" ad is a clear winner. On the other hand, serious questions have been raised about the testing process utilized. In defense of country image transfer, there was hardly enough repetition to realistically expect to achieve the conditioning which it requires. The other options mentioned are less compelling.

QUESTIONS
Guiding Questions

1. As an employee of the Alma Cheese Co., what constraints does Ms. Molke face as she attempts to develop an ad campaign for the U.S. market?

2. What are the main differences among the ads? Which differs more, the copy or the illustrations?

3. Which of the three prototype ads comes out best *overall* in the test reports provided in the case? What specific strengths *and* weaknesses does it show compared to the others?

4. What are "country of origin effects"? How can they help—or hinder— marketers seeking to export their brands?

5. What is the theory behind the "country image transfer" ad shown in Exhibit 20.3? What role does "emotional conditioning" play in this theory?

6. What is "portfolio testing"? What three criticisms of it are made in the case? Which of these do you think is the strongest given this particular business situation?

7. Would "focus groups" have been a more appropriate method for pretesting the three prototype ads? What advantage(s) do they have over "portfolio testing"? What disadvantage(s)?

8. What is the "Austrian Dilemma" which Alma is facing in this case? Is this a uniquely Austrian dilemma? Could it ever apply to a U.S. firm?

9. Was the sample of consumers suitable for the pretesting which Alma needed? What, if anything, would have made it a better sample?

10. In your own words, explain the argument advanced by Waltraud Iggers in the case? How much of it is rhetoric, and how much is substantive?

11. Do the pretest results support the ideas about emotional conditioning of country of origin effects which were developed by the researchers at the Economic University of Vienna?

Discussion Questions

1. What decision(s) do you think that Ms. Molke finally made? Be sure to explain carefully why you think *she* made them.

2. If you had been *in her place*, would you have made the same decision(s)? Why or why not?

3. While there is quite a bit of information provided in the case, what (if anything) else would *you* have wanted to know had you been in Ms. Molke's position?

4. Should Ms. Molke have followed the advice of the advertising creative, Ms. Iggers? Why or why not (Note: Ms. Iggers' view is quite common among people who actually create advertisements.)

5. Would the outcome of the testing have been different had the prototype ads been more polished? What differences in the illustration or copy of each ad might have made a difference?

6. Why do you think the results of the testing came out as they did? Would they have been different had the test been done in another part of the United States?

7. Would you have responded to the three ads the way most of the respondents did?

8. How much of a market should a firm like Alma realistically expect to gain in the United States? Given your answer, what should be the goal of Alma's advertising in the United States?

TEACHING TIPS

The case can be taught with different emphases according to the background and judgment of the instructor. There might be, for example, a focus on analyzing reported research results and critiquing various advertising research techniques. Or the focus might be upon the advertising environment of the modestly-sized firm—is Alma doomed to be a victim of the "double jeopardy effect" described by Ehrenberg et al. in the July 1990 issue of the *Journal of Marketing*? Alternatively, the focus might be on the tensions between research and creative people in advertising.

My own focus, which could go in tandem with any of the above, has been to involve students emotionally as well as rationally in the case. It is useful to call students to roleplay the roles of Rosawitha and Waltraud. Again, it is helpful to elicit from students empathetic reactions to the nightmare-like visions and misgivings which torture Ms. Molke as she tries to resolve an advertising strategy for the U.S. market. Some students may advocate tough-minded skepticism—but are shown that such a reaction leads one away from understanding the realistic pressures reported by many advertising people.

A NOTE ON PRONUNCIATION

The women's names in the case are typically Austrian. The letter "w" is pronounced like the English "v," "i" like "e." Hence, phonetically, "Rosa-*vee*-tha"; "*V*al-traud *Ee* ggers."

CASE 21

Magellan Luxury Travel*

TERENCE NEVETT

INTRODUCTION

In this case students are asked to assess the advertising policy of a small travel agency in the light of psychographic profiles developed by the Gallup Organization.

BACKGROUND

Magellan Travel has been operating successfully since 1977. Magellan's owner, Pamela Hall, is a travel enthusiast with a taste for exotic locations. She employs only people with a strong interest in travel. Mrs. Hall estimates that 75 percent of her business comes from vacation bookings, and Magellan is positioned at the luxury end of the market.

Magellan's advertising consists of mailings to current and former clients, and a weekly ad in the local newspaper. This ad is set in editorial style and describes the kind of exotic destinations that appeal to Mrs. Hall.

Magellan's clients are mostly in their fifties and sixties, and tend to book guided tours to routine tourist destinations. Independent travelers generally book cheap flights and moderately priced hotels. Clients tend to be well informed on travel related matters.

PROBLEM STATEMENT

Can Mrs. Hall use the Gallup psychographic profiles to improve the effectiveness of Magellan's advertising? If so, how?

Discussion

The seven dimensions are not directly relevant as far as Mrs. Hall is concerned, but are included to provide students with a fuller understanding of the research methodology. However, the profiles of the five groups provide interesting comparisons with Magellan's clients.

The current advertising seems to be appealing basically to adventurers. (Mrs. Hall herself probably falls into this category.) Some of the holidays she describes (beach holidays in Bali, castles in Spain) might also be attractive to indulgers, though the adventurer-oriented tone of the ads might strike a discordant note for them. However, Magellan is attracting clients who are well informed but actually book the more simple kinds of trips—in other words, dreamers. While they constitute a substantial segment of U.S. travelers (24 percent), they make fewer international trips.

Decision Options

Magellan Travel is operating successfully at present. However, there is a danger that a change to its advertising could upset the balance that seems to exist between creative appeal and client response. There may be a case for experimenting with the mailings, because it should be possible to identify traveler types from previous bookings and so tailor appeals to individual requirements. Even then such changes would have to be fairly subtle, so as to make certain that the image projected by the mailings did not conflict with that projected by the press ads.

The press advertising poses a more difficult problem. If Mrs. Hall changes it to appeal directly to the dreamers who seem to constitute her client base and to address their main concerns, then she will be changing fundamentally the character and tone of the ad, and thus the image projected by Magellan. This could well result in losing the dreamers, who probably gain a kind of vicarious pleasure from reading about exotic destinations and from dealing with an agency that makes that kind of booking.

PREFERRED OPTION

Mrs. Hall could carry out a controlled test with her mailings to see whether appeals targeted more closely to psychographic profiles produce an improved response. As far as the press advertising is concerned, however, she would probably be well advised to leave well enough alone. Magellan's success owes much to her personal enthusiasm which would be diminished if she had to write about subjects to which she could not relate.

Magellan seems to be well established in its own niche and to be suitably positioned. This should not be changed without good reason, and while the Gallup survey helps Mrs. Hall understand the motivations of different types of traveler, it does not provide any reason for altering the advertising.

QUESTIONS

Guiding Questions

To which of the psychographic groups is Magellan's advertising curently appealing?

What might be the advantages and disadvantages of changing (a) the mailings and/or (b) the press advertising?

Discussion Question

In general terms, how could the Gallup profiles be used in advertising?

TEACHING SUGGESTIONS

Students may well tend to focus on the research rather than the needs of Magellan. (They generally assume that an impressive piece of research is an indication that drastic change is required.) The profiles, although not directly relevant to Mrs. Hall's press advertising, can provide the basis for an interesting exercise in creating lifestyle-type campaigns in class. The instructor might begin by asking students to state which group each of them belongs to and to try and identify what kind of appeals might be effective in persuading them to use a particular travel agent.

CASE 22

Little Tykes Toy Company

JOHN M. SCHLEEDE

INTRODUCTION

Little Tykes allows the instructor to deal with the general issue of the opportunity for advertising and the specific issue of advertising's role in the marketing mix. In addition, the social issue of the appropriateness of advertising directed at children can be explored. Little Tykes has existed since its inception by **not** using advertising as its primary marketing tool, in contrast to the strategies employed by the market leaders. Although the company has been successful, new leadership is calling this policy into question.

OVERVIEW

Market Segments

It is clear from the discussion in the case, that there appear to be two distinct segments in the market, at least in the eyes of the major marketers.

Older children make up the first segment, and are perceived as having a major influence on both the products and the brands being purchased. As many parents and companies have found, to their chagrin, not purchasing the exact brand that the child wants will lead to disappointment for the child, dissatisfaction for parents, and ultimately to a lack of sales for the brands children are not looking for. Although many companies have copied Barbie, Barbie is the only doll of its type which remains on the market. The same could be said for G.I. Joe.

The second segment is made up of younger children, where the decision is much more that of the parents. Although children under the age of four or five may notice television commercials, strong brand loyalties and strong peer pressures still do not dominate the decision process. The parent remains the primary decision maker. The decision on which toy to purchcase is likely to involve extended problem solving behavior. In this case, the brand name acts as a cue, but does not necessarily guarantee purchase. The product's perceived suitability, relative price, etc., will be important considerations. Therefore, although a parent may trust Fisher Price or Little Tykes, there is no guarantee they will purchase that brand.

Competition

As there are two different markets, it would appear that competition is segmented as well. There is no question that the toy industry is dominated by the two giants: Hasbro and Mattel. The effects of changing demographics and the rising popularity of electronic games has caused the financial difficulties faced by second tier producers. Therefore, the toy industry finds itself with two big players for the older-kids market, with outsiders Nintendo, Sega, etc., siphoning off a large segment of the market.

For the younger children, the situation is not quite the same. Fisher Price has lost money, but is still a major player. Quaker Oats spinning off the brand may actually help it to prosper. Although Hasbro and Mattel are strong players in the preschool market, neither has the kind of dominance they exert in the older-age market. Little Tykes has continued to grow despite the general industry consolidation and low profit levels. Although this group has been affected by demographic trends, this market has not been affected by the electronic game industry. In a sense it might even be argued that the demographic changes have helped Little Tykes. Their products are relatively expensive, especially compared to Fisher Price, Mattel, etc. Therefore, if parents have fewer children it could be argued that they may well be willing to spend more per child.

PROBLEM STATEMENT

Should Little Tykes change their basic promotion strategy in order to accomplish their sales, profits, and market share goals?

Decision Options

1. Continue present promotional strategy and expenditure levels

2. Continue advertising exclusively to parents, but increase the level of expenditure to defend market share, while at the same time trying to retain the image of a small company that cares

3. Use television advertising targeted at children, perhaps linked to a popular TV program (Note the social and moral implications of such a move.)

Both (2) and (3) could be linked to aggressive promotion at retail level.

PREFERRED SOLUTION

Given that the target market that Little Tykes aims at is preschoolers, there is no reason to add any advertising aimed directly at children. However, there may be some reason to increase their advertising and promotional budgets. The product line has grown largely through word of mouth and satisfied, loyal consumers. The products themselves are sturdy plastic, which wears well and can really sell itself.

However, since parents are likely to use extended decision-making behavior, it could be argued that the company should take a more active role in creating awareness of its products and getting the parents to look at them in the store. Increased advertising of Little Tykes products in magazines targeted to parents would help to create basic awareness. Cooperative advertising or advertising and/or display allowances can be used to get parents into the store to look at the Little Tykes product line. This strategy would not be out of line with the company's basic philosophy, but would enable them to increase their sales and market share.

CASE 23

Michigan Lottery—Keno

TERENCE NEVETT

INTRODUCTION

Students are asked to outline planning decisions regarding target audience and message strategy. The data presented in the case are abstracted from much more detailed research reports, and the problem is posed in a rather simpler form than the one Barrera actually faced. His decision was complicated particularly by the interaction of Keno with Michigan's other lottery games, which is not mentioned here.

OVERVIEW

Ruben Barrera, Director of Research for the Michigan State Bureau of Lottery, is reviewing the findings of two surveys, one an annual tracking study of lottery play generally, and the other directed specifically to providing information about Keno play. The main findings are summarized in the case. Exhibits 23.2–23.9 contain data on lottery players, while Exhibits 23.10–23.15 detail responses to attitudinal questions on Keno.

PROBLEM STATEMENT

What recommendations should Barrera make about the promotion of Keno on the basis of the data provided?

Constraints

Budget: $750,000
Players: Must be 18+
Campaign: Must be statewide

Decision Options

This is not a simple case in which the decision maker is faced with a number of alternatives and has to choose between them. Barrera has to analyze carefully what is known about Keno's peformance to date to determine:

(a) whether there are any obvious weaknesses in Keno's position that advertising can rectify, and

(b) whether the game is perceived as having any attributes that could provide a creative platform.

There are a number of points that give cause for concern:

- The underlying rationale for lotteries in terms of the benefits for education and taxes does not seem to be widely understood.

- Keno does not seem to have been able to generate excitement. Players generally only find it mildly appealing.

- Non-players perceive Keno as confusing.

- In spite of positioning Keno as "the winning game," there is obviously considerable dissatisfaction about not winning, and a perception that the odds are bad.

- There has been a marked fall-off in Keno play.
  Note: This may not be as serious as it appears because free tickets were used to introduce the game, and these probably explain why some of the early players now play less. (This is not mentioned in the case, but could provide a lesson to students in not jumping to obvious conclusions.) However, free tickets probably do not provide the whole explanation, and there are two other possibilities to be considered. Either top-of-the-mind awareness is not being maintained (a promotional problem), or some of the players who tried Keno do not like it (a product problem). The latter explanation seems consistent with the number of complaints about not winning.

With regard to Keno's favorable attributes, there seems to be an absence of anything that could be used as the basis for an advertising campaign. Exhibit 23.15 shows that 40 percent of players and 66 percent of non-players either believe there are no favorable attributes or cannot think of any. The point most frequently mentioned—the better chance of winning—is something that many respondents clearly do not believe.

PREFERRED DECISION

Action seems to be needed on several fronts. The lack of understanding of what lottery income is used for clearly needs to be addressed. This is something that could affect the success not only of Keno but also of Michigan's other lottery games. There are arguments for running some form of informational campaign and/or building an informational element into advertising for the individual games, including Keno.

Unfavorable perceptions of Keno also need to be corrected. If the public do not believe the claim that Keno is "the winning game," then it must either be justified or abandoned.

The lack of excitement is consistent with the lack of a consensus regarding appealing elements of the game. It suggests the need for stronger positioning, showing Keno to be a low odds game that is fun and easy to play. The creative tone of the advertising can also help to create an aura of excitement. Since the amount wagered is the result of an impulse decision, this indicates a need for a powerful presence at point-of-purchase.

In the case, Barrera is also considering the target audience for Keno. Exhibits 23.2–23.9 show the demographic profile of lottery players to be similar to that of the Michigan population generally. The main exceptions are that more lottery players are married (Exhibit 23.4) and employed (Exhibit 23.6), while fewer professional people (Exhibit 23.3) or people on low incomes (Exhibit 23.9) are players. There is nothing remarkable here.

QUESTIONS
Guiding Questions

What are the significant points to come out of the research:

   (a) for lotteries generally?

   (b) for Keno in particular?

How could Barrera define the target audience for Keno?

Is it possible to use advertising to overcome the public's impression that the odds are unfavorable when playing Keno? If so, how?

How might excitement be built into Keno advertising?

What general message strategy should Barrera recommend?

Discussion Questions

What media could be used to reach potential Keno players?

Is there a need to differentiate betwee players and non-players in terms of creative appeals?

Are there any ethical or moral issues that arise when advertising lotteries?

WHAT ACTUALLY HAPPENED

It was decided to concentrate on strengthening Keno's position as the "winning" game, while at the same time using consumer promotions to generate enthusiasm. Advertising appeared on television and radio statewide in a series of three-week flights.

CASE 24

Peer Brothers Vacations*

TERENCE NEVETT

INTRODUCTION

The details in this case are based on an actual incident in which the company concerned suddenly came to undrestand the meaning of the term "damage control." The campaign described provides an interesting example of the benefits—and hazards—of using a linking motif in all advertising and promotional material.

BACKGROUND

Texas-based Peer Brothers specializes in travel to Southern Europe. The firm targets people visiting Europe for the first time and those who do not want the bother of making their own arrangements. Clients are mostly middle to upper-middle class Texans aged 45 plus. Peer Brothers offers friendly rather than luxury accommodation and puts heavy emphasis on service. Robert Peer runs the Texas headquarters, while Stephen spends most of his time in Europe.

Consumer advertising uses magazines and newspapers. The new campaign, created by agency Hendrick and Gladwyn, features (apparently) the two brothers, and a "brothers" motif is carried into print and miscellaneous promotional items. Peers do not use formal advertising research, but based on the rate of inquiries, Robert believes the new campaign to be working well.

After an unfortunate incident in Spain, Stephen is arrested. Robert receives a telephone call from a Spanish lawyer suggesting there may be diplomatic repercussions, and passing on a message from Stephen to cancel the "brothers" campaign.

PROBLEM STATEMENT

Should Robert cancel the "brothers" campaign as a damage control measure?

Constraints

- Time
  - Robert cannot do anything to limit the impact of the news that is about to break.
  - This is Peers' peak booking period.

- Information
  - Robert has no clear picture of how seriously the incident is likely to be viewed, either by the Spanish courts, or by Peer Brothers' own clients.

- Scope for change
  - Much of the campaign material is already prepared.

Decision Options

These points support a possible decision to continue with the "brothers" campaign:

- Peers have invested heavily in the campaign.

- The campaign seems to have been successful so far.

- Brochures, print items, etc., are already prepared, and it is too late to produce alternatives for the present season.

- Much of the color advertising is past cancellation date.

- The campaign will lose synergy if the motif is dropped.

- The personal association of the brothers with the firm is such that dropping the motif is likely to be of limited effect.

These points would support a decision to cancel the campaign:

- Clients may not wish to be associated with a firm, one of whose proprietors is at the center of an incident of this type.

- According to the Spanish lawyer, the incident is likely to receive wide media coverage.

- Confidence in the company generally could be undermined if Stephen is jailed.

- Limiting public exposure to the "brothers" motif could help limit the damage of Stephen's association with the firm.

PREFERRED OPTION

There are considerable risks in either case. If Robert does nothing and lets the "brothers" campaign continue, the firm may suffer from association with a widely publicized international incident. If he cancels, there is likely to be a drop in revenue because no advertising appears at peak booking time.

Timing of the decision is important. There is nothing Robert can do to put a favorable spin on the news, and there is no point in considering any further action until Stephen has appeared in court and the outcome is known. In the meantime, Robert should probably refuse any requests for media interviews on the grounds that he is awaiting clarification of the situation from Spain. Based on the information available to him that morning, the implications of cancellation seem more serious than those of letting the campaign continue, but this could change when the results of Stephen's court appearance are known.

QUESTIONS
Guiding Questions

Should Robert make a decision about cancellation immediately, or is there anything to be gained by waiting? If so, for how long?

Is removal of the "brothers" motif likely to be effective in diverting public attention away from Stephen's connection with the firm?

To what extent would it be practical to delete the motif?

Discussion Questions

What are the benefits of using a motif such as the "brothers" across a range of advertising and promotional materials?

How seriously would an incident like the one described be regarded in your (students') local community? Would attitudes differ across age groups and/ or social classes?

WHAT ACTUALLY HAPPENED

The details of Stephen's court appearance are somewhat sketchy. It seems, however, that he made a lengthy and profound apology, paid a fine, was cautioned by the judge as to his future conduct, and walked from the court a free man. The story was picked up by the media, but there was less attention paid to it than the brothers had feared. The focus in the coverage was not so much on the diplomatic implications as on the item of underwear and were it had come from. The reaction of the firm's clients seemed to be one of mild amusement—"Boys will be boys." The "brothers" campaign continued to run and bookings seemed unaffected.

CASE 25

N.Z. Kiwifruit Authority (B)

Charles H. Patti and Shengliang Deng

INTRODUCTION

Background

The two versions of this case were developed as a result of visiting professorships by Shengliang Deng and me at Otago University in Dunedin, New Zealand. Sheng and I did not know each other before our visits to Dunedin, but we arrived on the same day, and within a couple of weeks we discovered some mutual interests in marketing in New Zealand. Given the relatively short time I was going to be in New Zealand (6 months), I knew it was going to be difficult to launch a major research project. At the same time, I wanted to get to know more about New Zealand marketing. I have been interested and active in case development for many years, and when I began to learn about the importance of kiwifruit to New Zealand, I decided to contact the New Zealand Kiwifruit Authority (NZKA) to learn more. Eventually, Sheng and I decided to work together to develop a case that would help students understand the global marketing issues involved in this unusual product.

We gathered a lot of information about kiwifruit from the NZKA, from kiwifruit marketing boards and agencies throughout the world and from libraries and public records. After analyzing all of the information, we decided that the two most interesting issues facing the NZKA were branding and advertising. This version of the case deals with advertising creative strategy.

Needed Background of the Student

One aspect I like best in using cases is that you can work with them at several different levels. For example, I created this version with advanced advertising students in mind—specifically those who are enrolled in advertising management, advertising campaigns, or advertising creative strategy. However, I have used the case effectively with an audience that had no prior advertising course experience. So, your choice of how deeply you want the issues analyzed will determine the required student background.

OVERVIEW OF THE CASE

Kiwifruit is a very odd-looking fruit that is most associated with New Zealand, but in fact was originated in China. The highly nutritious fruit was brought to New Zealand and eventually marketed successfully—first within New Zealand, then to Australia and England, and eventually to world-wide markets.

As the market for kiwifruit expanded, the New Zealand Kiwifruit Authority was formed to compile information about the market and to facilitate the exporting and marketing of the product. For many years, New Zealand owned the small but steady kiwifruit market. Partially because the worldwide market for kiwifruit was never huge and because competition was virtually non-existent, the NZKA did not brand the product, nor did they protect the name "kiwifruit." Promotion largely consisted of small point-of-purchase materials and a few studies to document the nutritional value of kiwifruit.

Eventually, this changed. Competition developed from the United States, Chile, and Italy. These countries also produced a high-quality kiwifruit and began to promote their product aggressively. NZKA countered with increased promotion, including providing advertising and point-of-purchase assistance to marketing boards throughout the world. Nevertheless, New Zealand lost market share, and by this time, the overall volume of kiwifruit sales was significant. Therefore, the successful marketing of kiwifruit became very important to the New Zealand economy.

PROBLEM STATEMENT

The NZKA—and the various international kiwifruit marketing boards throughout the world—have tried a number of promotion themes. (Examples of these approaches are illustrated in the case.) At the end of the case, the student is confronted by two related problems:

- Which creative strategy should the NZKA use in its advertising?

- Should the NZKA adopt a single, global advertising strategy?

Constraints

Financial

The case does not specifically mention many constraints; however, many students—particularly those who have had several courses in advertising and marketing—should realize that New Zealand is a relatively small country (approximately three million people) and not a particularly wealthy country. Therefore, the amount of funds available to promote kiwifruit will be limited. The growth in advertising and promotion spending is documented in the case, and although the increases have been significant, the overall amount is not enormous.

Geographic

The stucture of the NZKA and the worldwide distribution and marketing of kiwifruit limit the control that the NZKA will have on implementing any particular advertising strategy. Eventually, each country controls how it will sell kiwifruit, and the case is filled with examples that illustrate the diversity of advertising approaches.

Marketing Expertise

The marketing history of kiwifruit is short on advertising and promotion. The international marketing of kiwifruit was an afterthought. Traditionally, there has been much more attention paid to packing, shipping, and pricing than to advertising or promotion. Certainly, New Zealand is capable of producing effective advertising; however, focusing attention on kiwifruit advertising has not been the primary thrust of the NZKA.

Competition

The effectiveness of any particular creative strategy also depends on the efforts of the competition, specifically the kiwifruit advertising of the United States, Chile, and Italy. The United States and Italy are particularly aggressive and skilled at advertising; therefore, the NZKA will have to anticipate the competitive response of these marketers.

Decision Options

There are two primary issues in this case. The first one deals with the selection of a creative strategy. The decision options in this issue are clearly laid out. There are three alternative creative strategies provided, and most students are going to select from among these three. However, some students will think of other alternatives, and indeed they should be encouraged to do so.

The second issue raised in the case—whether the NZKA should launch a global advertising theme—forces students to think about the alternative: allow each country in which New Zealand kiwifruit is marketed to develop its own advertising theme.

Within the case—specifically in Exhibit 25.17 "Summary of Alternative Creative Strategy Themes Under Consideration by the NZKA"—there are rationales and analyses for each of the three provided alternatives. The three provided alternatives are:

- Theme A: "Buy NZ kiwifruit because it is healthy, nutritious, and tasty."

Rationale and Analysis: This is essentially the generic theme used by the NZKA for many years. It focuses on the fruit's main selling features: its several impressive physical attributes. Research has shown that the main reasons that people eat kiwifruit are the enjoyment of its taste and its place as an alternative to less healthy foods.

Those who feel it is time to move away from this theme point out that the competitive nature of the marketplace means that New Zealand must create a differential advantage, and the generic theme does little beyond selling kiwifruit in general. Some even felt that this theme is now largely the cause of the increased success of New Zealand's competitors who are benefitting from the awareness and educational tasks accomplished by NZKA advertising.

- Theme B: "'Buy NZ kiwifruit because it is the original kiwifruit, and it comes from a beautiful, charming country."

Rationale and Analysis: Associating kiwifruit with the overall, favorable image of New Zealand as a largely untouched paradise with friendly, healthy people is a natural, easy way to create a distinct image for New Zealand's kiwifruit. Several recent studies have confirmed the attractiveness of New Zealand: the country consistently earns high rankings in "places I'd most like to visit." Furthermore, more people associate kiwifruit with New Zealand than with any other country despite the fact that "kiwifruit" is not a brand name of New Zealand.

Those arguing against adopting this theme point out that the other major producers of kiwifruit (Italy, Chile, and the United States) can also link their product to the physical beauty of their respective countries. No one denies that New Zealand is beautiful, but those arguing against Theme B warn that promoting kiwifruit essentially on the basis of its association with the physical beauty of New Zealand will only prompt other countries to adopt a similar strategy, thus leaving New Zealand still without a differential advantage.

- Theme C: "Buy NZ kiwifruit because it is a distinctive personality."

Rationale and Analysis: Several members of the committee felt that the key to advertising success is to create a distinctive personality for New Zealand kiwifruit that uses a spokesperson (well-known sports personality, for example) or brand character (along the lines of the Jolly Green Giant, Charlie the Tuna, or the Pillsbury Doughboy). Their idea is that the spokesperson or brand character will give the product its own, distinctive personality, and at the same time it will communicate the want-satisfying benefits of the fruit's physical attributes.

There was considerable discussion about this option and those arguing against it pointed out two major, potential problems. First, spokespersons are risky. Athletes and entertainment personalities, for example, can easily lose their appeal, and if this happens, the product image will suffer significantly. Second, it is expensive and time-consuming to launch a successful brand character. It usually takes ten years or more and millions of dollars of advertising and promotion effort to communicate a distinctive and desirable personality for a brand character. It is doubtful that the increasingly competitive nature of the marketplace will give New Zealand the time and financial resources to develop a brand character.

PREFERRED DECISION

Our preferred decision is Theme C, the distinctive personality approach. While all three themes have promise, we like Theme C because:

- It seems to fit best within the constraints explained above.

- It will allow each country that markets New Zealand kiwifruit to adapt the theme to its own environment—that is, each country can select a spokesperson who is attractive to the local market.

- It is most difficult to copy by the competitors (United States, Italy, and Chile).

If you want to consider the use of Theme C as a global advertising strategy with local adaptations, then perhaps the answer to the global advertising issue is yes—develop a global strategy. However, we do not recommend a single, global strategy for the NZKA at this time, largely because of the constraints mentioned above and because the two best alternatives for a single, global strategy (Themes A and B) are so generic that it is unlikely that either will provide the NZKA with a competitive advantage.

QUESTIONS
Guiding Questions

What creative strategy options do you see for the NZKA?

What is your opinion on the three options they are currently considering?

Do you think the NZKA should adopt a global advertising theme?

What is your recommendation for a creative strategy for the NZKA? Why?

Discussion Questions

What factors most influence the selection of creative strategy for the NZKA?

When compared with other promotion tools, how important do you feel advertising is in the marketing success of kiwifruit for New Zealand?

WHAT ACTUALLY HAPPENED?

All of the information in this case is authentic with the exception of the current situation section—that is, as far as we know, the NZKA is not considering alternative creative strategies or a global strategy. After analyzing all of the information we found about the NZKA, we felt that they should be evaluating issues; however, we have no specific information that they are doing so. Therefore, we don't know what actually happened. Our experience with case writing and case teaching is that some students want to know "what actually happened," so the lack of an answer might be frustrating for some of them. When the "what actually happened" is not known, I always tell students this before they start their analysis so they will not become further frustrated by trying to contact the subject company or spending hours or days in the library looking for the "right answer."

TEACHING TIPS

The marketing of produce is something that students don't often think about, yet it is a very interesting area for study. There have been some notable successes and failures, and students should be encouraged to spend some time thinking about both. For example, have students do some research on the marketing of Dole and Chiquita produce. These are two brands that have done quite well for the most part. However, students who research these brands will also discover the failure to brand and advertise Chiquita lettuce. Similarly, Morton Salt has been very successfully advertised, yet most other marketers of physically undifferentiated products have not been very successful. What is responsible for these successes and failures? What role has advertising played? And, can any particular advertising creative strategy really bring about the success of a product like New Zealand kiwifruit? After all, New Zealand kiwifruit is not significantly superior to its competitors' offerings.

   In addition to the stimulating class discussion about these issues, this case should also encourage students to collect and examine the advertising of Dole, Chiquita, DelMonte, and others. Ask students to classify the advertising creative strategies of these companies, comparing the strategies to those under consideration by the NZKA.

   Finally, this case provides a good opportunity to organize your class into three groups, each advocating one of the strategies of the NZKA. You can have the three groups present their reasons for advocating their theme to the entire class for discussion and evaluation.

REFERENCES

A very useful reading to accompany this case is "Creative Strategy: A Management Perspective," by Charles F. Frazer, *Journal of Advertising*, 12:4 (1983), 36–41. This article also provides much of the basis of Chapter 12, Developing Creative Strategy, in *Advertising: A Decision-Making Approach*, by Charles H. Patti and Charles F. Frazer, The Dryden Press, Hinsdale, Illinois, 1988. The *JA* article—and particularly Chapter 12 of the Patti & Frazer book—provides students with alternative creative strategies and their potential effectiveness under different market conditions.

United Chemical Products

Terence Nevett

INTRODUCTION

This case raises two issues that may arise at some point in an advertising manager's career. One is the position of an advertiser when a publication on the media schedule runs an unfavorable story. (This raises the broader question of the relationship between advertising and the freedom of the press.) The other is the position of the advertising manager who is instructed by a superior to take an action that conflicts with a strongly held belief or personal principle.

BACKGROUND

The company has launched a corporate image campaign that is appearing in the *Wall Street Journal* and selected business publications. The aim of the campaign is to improve the company's image and restore public confidence after what its CEO refers to as "a few unfortunate incidents," which include some involvement in the dumping of toxic waste. The CEO has approved the campaign theme and the media strategy. Now, however, he wants to pull United Chemical's ads from the *Wall Street Journal* because it has published an article critical of the company. Since he does not question the accuracy of the article, it may be assumed to be justified.

PROBLEM STATEMENT

The advertising manager must decide whether to obey the CEO's instruction, with which he strongly disagrees, and if not, decide what alternative course of action he should take.

Constraints

- The CEO's view that the advertiser – media relationship is no different from any other buyer – seller relationship

- The CEO's short temper

- The likely response of the *Wall Street Journal* to attempts to bring pressure to bear on its editorial coverage

- The effect that deleting the *Journal* from the media schedule will have on United Chemical's media strategy and thus on their campaign objectives.

Decision Options

The advertising manager can follow the CEO's instructions and pull the campaign. This might be prudent, given the CEO's temper and the manager's presumed desire to keep his job. Students faced with this situation will often see the choice as lying between acceptance or resignation. If they are asked to imagine themselves in the role of Bruck, however, and to think through the implications of an action they believe to be incorrect and which goes against their personal principles, they will tend to start looking for a way out of the predicament.

A compromise solution would be to follow the instruction for the moment, let the heat die down, and then approach the CEO with a more reasoned argument. Bruck was caught off guard and did not marshal his arguments very well. In a calmer setting, having had time to prepare his case, he might do rather better. In particular, he could point out what the reaction of the *Journal* might be to what seems like a clumsy attempt to influence editorial policy. If that were given editorial coverage, it could do considerable harm to the company's already tarnished image.

Bruck could reinforce his position by calling in help. The agency would be the obvious ally in this situation, since trying to negotiate media buys with strings attached would put them in an impossible position. Their top management would probably be willing to meet with Wells, to explain to him that the advertising business does not operate in the way he seems to believe. They could also reinforce the target audience implications of deleting the *Journal* from the schedule.

PREFERRED DECISION

Bruck has justice on his side, even though his case was not very well expressed. It is reasonable, therefore, for him to fight for his beliefs, and not to sacrifice them to expediency. The question then becomes one of how and when to fight. Given the general tone of his argument with Wells, there seems little point in a further confrontation that morning, which might even put his job in jeopardy. Rather than outright cancellation of further insertions in the *Journal*, they could be put on hold for the time being. A meeting could then be arranged at which Bruck, the agency, and any allies he could muster within the company could present their arguments to Wells. Although company structure is not mentioned in the case, Bruck would presumably have a superior at vice-president level who could be called on to help.

QUESTIONS
Guiding Questions

To what extent is Wells correct in stating that money allocated to the *Wall Street Journal* could now be spent more effectively in other publications?

Are there any further arguments that Bruck could use to make his case?

Should a newspaper withhold unfavorable editorial coverage of its advertisers?

Discussion Questions

Is Bruck a theorist living in an unreal world?

Can an advertiser treat media in the same way as other suppliers?

If people like Wells were able to control what coverage was given them by the media, would this represent an ultimate threat to democracy in this country?

WHAT ACTUALLY HAPPENED

Bruck was not politically adroit and failed to rally any support for his case within the company. He complied with Wells' instructions but was very unhappy about the whole episode. Subsequently, he took early retirement and went to live abroad.

TEACHING SUGGESTIONS

Students typically see Bruck's alternatives as compliance or resignation. They may need to be guided into considering how Bruck could strengthen his position politically, how he could buy time, and the possibility of some kind of compromise. (Wells is unlikely to accept any proposal that causes him to lose face.) The conflict between the advertising manager's need to spend money in the most effective way and the media's right to free speech usually generates lively debate.

CASE 27

Trees Atlanta's Crossroads

CATHY J. COBB – WALGREN

INTRODUCTION

This case deals with strategic marketing issues facing a nonprofit organization. As such, it provides a useful point of departure for comparing and contrasting marketing in the private (for profit) sector with marketing in the public (nonprofit) sector. Students will gain experience in analyzing the situation, setting objectives, choosing a target, and developing general marketing communication strategy. Students should be familiar with the four types of persuasive marketing communication: advertising, sales promotion, public relations, and personal selling. Also, students should have a good understanding of consumer behavior and marketing research, since they will be asked to evaluate the results of a consumer research project in the course of making recommendations.

BACKGROUND

Trees Atlanta is a nonprofit, citizen's group dedicated to preserving and planting trees in the metropolitan Atlanta area. In addition to saving old trees and planting new ones, Trees Atlanta is involved in educating business, government, and consumer groups on tree-related issues, lobbying for tree protection ordinances, and administering tree donor programs. Founded in 1984, the organization has grown in size from a handful of concerned citizens to 600 members by mid-1991. Since its founding, Trees Atlanta has been instrumental in planting almost 65,000 trees. Despite this success, there are many problems and opportunities which lie ahead. First of all, Atlanta is at risk of losing its status as the most heavily forested urban region of the country because of unprecedented tree loss, due primarily to encroaching development. Then, too, fully half of Atlanta's 2.6 million population has never heard of Trees Atlanta. The organization's work thus far has focused mainly on business and government groups.

PROBLEM STATEMENT

Students are asked to evaluate Trees Atlanta's current situation, including an examination of the results of a marketing research study. They are then expected to make recommendations in the following areas: target market, communication objectives, potential sources of funding, general marketing communication strategy, and specific creative tone of the marketing communication campaign.

Constraints

1. *Lack of financial resources*. Trees Atlanta operates on an annual budget of only $150.000, which comes from corporations, foundations, and individual contributions. This money is used to purchase trees, pay the salary of the director, print and mail newsletters, conduct educational seminars, and other administrative expenses. There is very little left over for funding a marketing communication campaign.

2. *Shortage of staff*. Despite a membership of 600, Trees Atlanta has only one paid staffperson—Ms. Bansley. She works out of a small, donated office in a downtown office building. There is not sufficient office space to maintain a large staff. And without additional staff members to man telephones, update mailing lists, field questions, etc., Ms. Bansley is worried that a successful, large-scale membership drive could overwhelm the organization.

3. *Potentially conflicting loyalties*. Trees Atlanta is in a delicate position as an environmental organization which must rely on government and business for cooperation. Historically, these two groups have *not* been considered environmentally conscious. Thus, Ms. Bansley must avoid positioning Trees Atlanta as an extremist environmental group (such as Greenpeace). Otherwise, she risks alienating mainstream, conservative Atlantans. At the same time, she must avoid the perception that Trees Atlanta is under the control of powerful pro-business groups, for then she would jeopardize the integrity of the organization.

Analysis of the Marketing Research Study

In evaluating the research design, students should observe that the sample size (N = 400) is adequate. The response rate (52 percent) is also acceptable for a telephone survey, given the number of answering machines in operation and the amount of telemarketing activity in the area. Students could compare census data from the library with the sample characteristics presented in Exhibit 27.4. If they did, they would discover that the sample is slightly older and better educated than the general population of Atlanta and somewhat more likely to be white. But the differences are not great.

Listed below are some of the key findings which students should glean from Exhibits 27.5 through 27.12.

1. The environment is not as important to Atlantans as the social issues of education, drugs, and crime. But then, Atlanta hasn't had the environmental problems that more industrialized regions of the country have had to face. Remember, too, that the South is a conservative region which needs to encourage economic development and, thus, is more likely to be fairly lax in its environmental restrictions. The irony is that, eventually, the pro-development atmosphere is going to create environmental problems, unless there is a concerted effort by government, business, and consumer groups to head off these problems.

2. Atlantans' level of concern for various environments is bimodal. At one extreme, people are concerned with the global environment. At the other extreme, they are concerned about their immediate neighborhood. There is less concern for metro and state environments. This represents a potential problem *and* opportunity for Trees Atlanta.

3. Unaided recall of Trees Atlanta is extremely low. The organization received only 8 mentions when respondents were asked to name any environmental groups they could think of. Not surprisingly, Greenpeace received the most mentions. But it is in the news regularly, and it conducts regular fundraising campaigns. It is telling that the second most frequent response was "other." This demonstrates how fragmented the responses were.

4. Over half of the sample responded "don't know" to the question about Trees Atlanta's overall effectiveness. Students may consider this a problem, but it is really more of an opportunity. It is much harder to counter negative opinions than to build or maintain positive ones. (Indeed, it has been said that it takes 12 positive exposures to counter one negative exposure.) The fact that only 7 percent of the sample felt that Trees Atlanta is doing a poor job is encouraging.

5. The more people know about Trees Atlanta, the more they perceive its role as teaching developers and lobbying government. It could be that this is where Trees Atlanta gets most of its press.

Decision Options

The major decision areas are given below, followed by a listing of the pros and cons of each alternative.

Target Market

Consumers

(+) Consumers represent an untapped market. Half of the sample had never heard of Trees Atlanta.

(+) Consumers as a group are generally pro-environment.

(+) Atlantans are very proud of their city; there is a high level of booster-ism. Thus, it may be an easy sell.

(+) Zoo Atlanta, another local nonprofit group, has experienced phenomenal success targeting consumers.

(−) It would be very expensive and potentially wasteful to pursue an undifferentiated segmentation strategy. As the research revealed, not all Atlantans are concerned about the environment.

(−) Related to this, it would be time consuming and expensive to locate those consumers who would be the most responsive to environmental issues. Students should note, however, that it *can* be done with the existing data base. Depending on the variables included in the data analysis, Trees Atlanta researchers could use cluster analysis, regression, or discriminant analysis to identify pro-environmental groups. Then they could match these group members with zip codes, and blanket the most favorable zip code areas with a direct mail campaign.

(−) As a group, consumers give small donations relative to businesses.

(−) It may be difficult to get consumers to perceive that there is a problem (given all of the existing trees in the Atlanta area).

(−) It may also be difficult to get consumers to believe that they as individuals can make a difference.

Business

(+) The business community has the financial clout that consumers do not.

(+) Because the business community is a smaller group than consumers, it is easier to target and reach this group.

(+) In a related sense, because businesses represent a smaller target, it is more feasible to make personal sales calls.

(+) From experience, Ms. Bansley knows that businesses would prefer not to go head-to-head with city and county governments in fighting restrictive tree-planting policies (e.g., it is not always easy to get city approval to plant trees along the sidewalks surrounding an office building). Instead, they would rather have an organization like Trees Atlanta fight their battles for them. Money is not the issue; bureaucratic red tape is. Most companies are only too happy to give generous donations in return for this favor.

(+) Donating to Trees Atlanta is an easy way for businesses to exercise (and get recognition for) their civic responsibility.

(+) Only the major corporations in Atlanta have been targeted by Trees Atlanta to date. Small businesses have not been tapped.

(−) As noted above, the business community does not represent a new target for Trees Atlanta. It is not clear how much additional revenue can be gained from this group.

(−) Historically, businesses (particularly developers) have not been very pro-environment.

(−) Many companies are feeling the economic pinch and may not be willing or able to take on another philanthropic activity.

Government

(+) City and county governments are responsible for many ordinances which govern the cutting and planting of trees.

(−) A tight state budget leaves few resources for beautification projects.

(−) Some government offices (such as the DOT) already have landscaping programs.

Types of Marketing Communication Activities

The idea is to encourage students to brainstorm on low-cost/no-cost ways to publicize Trees Atlanta and thereby further its mission. The principal rule of brainstorming is to defer judgment. So, caution students not to judge ideas too quickly. Listed below are some of the ideas (of course, not all were used) Trees Atlanta came up with:

1. Tree Ts—sponsor a contest among school-age children for the best drawing of what trees mean to them. Put the winning drawing on T-shirts and sell them.

2. Make a calendar of kindergarten students' drawings of Atlanta's landscape.

3. Tree Mobile—Get a local car dealership to loan a van, which would serve as a traveling office/museum for Trees Atlanta. The tree mobile could make stops at area schools, parks, events, etc.

4. Write a weekly column for the newspaper on tree-related issues. The format could be question/answer.

5. Print messages on area supermarket bags.

6. Give an annual award to the residential and/or commercial developer who does the most to conserve trees.

7. Get neighborhood/subdivision associations involved in beautification projects. Give an award to the neighborhood which does the most to plant and preserve trees.

8. Enlist the efforts of local radio and television stations in producing and airing a public service announcement.

9. Get the telephone company to donate and publicize a telephone hotline number, where callers can hear timely tree-related messages (such as fall tree-planting tips).

10. Regularly saturate the media with press releases.

11. Enlist the efforts of churches (e.g., put messages in church bulletins).

12. Offer a matching program to corporations for planting trees (i.e., the company plants a tree, and Trees Atlanta plants one).

13. Participate in Earth Day, the annual flower show, and other relevant events.

14. Work with local boy scout and girl scout troups to promote tree care.

Sources of Funding

Once again, the key is to get students to be creative in identifying ways to fund a campaign. For example, the following groups often do pro bono creative work: local agencies, university marketing/advertising departments, university small business development centers, professional trade schools (such as Atlanta's Portfolio Center), local ad clubs, and the Ad Council (although it limits projects to those which are national in scope). In addition, media space and time could be donated by local media organizations. Printing firms could donate materials and labor for actual production. Local radio and TV talent could be enlisted to perform or act as spokespersons. (The instructor should note that Trees Atlanta used all of the above as sources of funding.)

One last option for increasing Trees Atlanta revenues would be to change the one-time membership fee to an annual fee.

Tone of the Campaign

The instructor is referred to the vast literature on fear appeals as a point of departure for discussing the desired tone of the marketing communication campaign. Basically, there are two options: a positive, upbeat tone which focuses on Atlanta's beauty and the success of Trees Atlanta, and a more negative, somber approach which emphasizes the current level of tree loss in Atlanta and the ramifications of doing nothing to offset this trend. Students should list the pros and cons of each alternative. For example, one reason not to use the positive approach is that it may lull the audience into complacency. As noted earlier, negative information carries more weight than positive information. On the other hand, a negative approach could result in the audience putting up perceptual defenses to avoid dealing with the issue.

The literature on fear appeals suggests that strong attitudes do not always translate into behavior. So, the fact that many Atlantans are pro-environment doesn't mean necessarily that they will join Trees Atlanta.

Unfortunately, too, most people do not think that the benefits of environmentally-conscious actions outweigh the costs. This is a real dilemma for Trees Atlanta, particularly if the organization targets individuals. The primary reason is that the costs (of joining, donating, lobbying, etc.) accrue to the individual. But the benefits are primarily to the group. For people to engage in specific behaviors (such as planting a tree or donating to Trees Atlanta), they need to feel that their actions will make a difference. The tone of any Trees Atlanta communication should emphasize that one individual *can* make a difference.

QUESTIONS
Guiding Questions

1. What target or targets should Trees Atlanta pursue?

2. What specific marketing communication tools should Trees Atlanta utilize?

3. How should the marketing communication program be funded?

4. What should the tone of the marketing communication be?

Discussion Questions

1. How is the marketing of a nonprofit organization similar to that of a for-profit business? How is it different?

2. How should a firm decide which types of marketing communication to use and how much weight to assign to each?

WHAT ACTUALLY HAPPENED

Trees Atlanta decided to pursue the business community as a target. The major tools used were sales calls, press releases, a direct-mail piece (the goal of which was to create awareness, educate the target, and promote action in the form of a contribution), and a sales support packet with pockets for inserts which could be tailor-made for each company (as a leave-behind following the sales pitch by Ms. Bansley). In addition, a special program was designed to increase involvement among small businesses (e.g., they could buy half a tree). All of the communication materials were produced and printed at no cost to Trees Atlanta by local firms. Mailing costs for the direct mail piece were nominal, since the nonprofit postage rate was used.

The main reason for choosing the business target was that businesses give much higher donations than individuals. Thus, it was felt that a full-fledged campaign among *all* Atlanta-area business (not just the piecemeal approach which had been used to date) would raise enough revenues to support a consumer campaign the following year. In addition, it was felt that the business campaign, particularly if it enlisted employees as well as employers, would build legitimacy for Trees Atlanta before the organization took its case to the general public.

The theme for the campaign was "Trees Atlanta—Shading the Present, Shaping the Future." The tone was lively and positive. There were no accusations, no 1970s-style ecological preaching, no negatives, and no direct confrontation. However, the communication did have a serious undercurrent to remind the audience that Trees Atlanta means business (no pun intended).

FURTHER READINGS

Kotler, Philip, O.C. Ferrell, and Charles Lamb (1987). *Strategic Marketing for Nonprofit Organizations: Cases and Readings*, Englewood Cliffs, NJ: Prentice – Hall.

Rothschild, Michael L. (1979). "Marketing Communications in Nonbusiness Situations or Why It's So Hard to Sell Brotherhood Like Soap," *Journal of Marketing*, 43 (Spring), 11–20.

CASE 28

Marfio's Tijuana Takeout*

TERENCE NEVETT

INTRODUCTION

People who have been laid off often manifest a strong desire to be self-employed, and so invest their savings in some small business about which they know nothing. In Tijuana Takeout, students are asked to relate the potential contribution of advertising (of which the owner has no experience) to the needs and resources of the business.

BACKGROUND

Having been laid off, Joe Marfio opts to open a Mexican fast-food outlet positioned upmarket from Taco Bell.

Fast Food:
- It is the fastest growing area of eating place sales, with sales forecast to exceed $74 billion in 1991.

- Although sales are slower than in the seventies and early eighties, the industry believes the economic downturn will work in their favor.

- Taco Bell is the fastest growing fast food chain in terms of sales per unit, which now average $800,000.

Tijuana Takeout:
- The site is on the interstate one mile from other fast food outlets (but is only likely to get drivers traveling east).

- The emphasis is on takeout; the interior and service are very basic.

- Target markets are:
  - Passing trade on interstate (but no truck parking)
  - Used car dealers (lunch)
  - Business people (lunch)
    Note: delivery service not available at lunchtime.
  - Local residents

Tijuana Promotion:

- Leaflets delivered to every household.

- Radio spots to announce opening.

- Newspaper ad to announce opening.

- Publicity in local newspaper.

- Sign on Tijuana building.

- Copy confined to menu items and prices.

- Marfio planned to spend 3 percent of sales in first year, scaling back to 2 percent in second

PROBLEM STATEMENT

The immediate problem is whether Marfio should take the sign being offered by Krantz. However, there is a more fundamental problem of whether ineffective advertising is really the reason for Tijuana's failure to meet sales forecasts.

Decision Options

These will depend on the extent to which advertising is considered responsible for Marfio's problems.

Reasons why advertising may be at fault:
Advertising does not seem to have gained attention, and was not remembered—customers could not recall it.

Radio spot seems to have sounded like the menu read by an amateur.

Nothing was designed to get prospects to try the menu—no coupons, special offers, etc.

Alternative explanations for lack of repeat business:
The buying cycle is longer than forecast.

Variety seekers try it once but are basically Taco Bell customers.

Customer dissatisfaction because:

- The interior is not authentic Mexican.

- Higher prices may not be justified if customers cannot perceive any difference from Taco Bell.

- They may not be happy with food quality; is it really authentic Mexican when it comes out of a microwave pack?

- Menu items may not be attractive; Marfio offers different items from Taco Bell to justify price differential, but Taco Bell's menu is what people know and like.

Lack of new customers:
Tijuana is in a poor location at wrong end of town.

The image is confusing, changing from Mexican to American after a few weeks.

There is no incentive to sample.

There may be too many fast food outlets for a small town to support. (Marfio only knows national figures, not how successful they are locally.)

Preferred Option

This will depend on where students think the fault lies. Realistically, all the points made above are valid and require attention, but since Marfio is operating with extremely limited resources, priorities have to be established. It seems logical to make certain first that the offering is correct. Otherwise, new customers he manages to attract are likely not to return. Both in terms of his menu and his advertising, Marfio needs to bear in mind that he is positioned against Taco Bell and give Taco Bell customers a reason for trying his more expensive offering.

Given Tijuana's current position, there is a need for any further promotion to be action-oriented. Some incentive to sample such as a coupon would draw customers into the store, while a loyalty promotion would help to build up routine patronage. Krantz's sign is really irrelevant. Funds would be better expended on trying to build up a loyal customer base in the town than on attracting passing trade.

QUESTIONS
Guiding Questions

What other factors apart from ineffective advertising might be responsible for Tijuana Takeout's poor performance? What steps might be taken to rectify the situation?

What improvements could Marfio make to (a) his use of media, and (b) the content of his advertising?

Should Marfio accept the sign being offered by Krantz?

Is percentage of forecast sales a suitable method of setting the advertising budget for Tijuana?

Discussion Question

Are there any steps that someone in Marfio's position (that is to say, laid off and wishing to start their own business) could reasonably take to avoid making the same mistakes in promotion?

WHAT ACTUALLY HAPPENED

Marfio eventually decided to close the business and conserve what remained of his savings.

TEACHING SUGGESTIONS

Students working on this case usually assume that as they are sitting in an advertising management class, they are being called upon to develop proposals for improving Tijuana's advertising. It may need to be pointed out to them that if the basic premise upon which the business was started was incorrect, no amount of advertising that Marfio can afford would be able to correct the situation. They should therefore focus on whether there is any contribution that advertising can make before they consider what that contribution might be. Role play between Marfio and Krantz is a useful way of identifying factors related to the sign.

CASE 29

Neat 'N Tidy: Fine Accessories

TERRENCE H. WITKOWSKI

INTRODUCTION

The case asks students to think along with Mary Schaefer as she formulates the marketing plan for her Neat 'N Tidy catalog and projects its costs and revenues.

In addition to the material that describes the factors behind and the practice of catalog and mail-order marketing, the case presents some of the elements of a new business plan including a company situation analysis, a marketing strategy, and a sales and profit forecast.

BACKGROUND

Mary Schaefer is a 43-year-old mother of two, with an MBA and experience as a marketing research analyst. She operates two successful retail stores and is now considering moving into catalog sales, an area that is showing dramatic growth.

This highly flexible combination of direct response advertising and non-store retailing offers consumers a level of shopping convenience and product assortment that often cannot be matched through conventional channels. Direct marketing systems, in general, enable sellers to carefully select target audiences, personalize offerings, build customer relationships, test messages and media, and measure response.

PROBLEM STATEMENT

The overall problem in this case is whether and how a successful, but small retail operation should take its product assortment nationwide through direct response and catalog advertising. The immediate problem raised at the end of the case concerns Mary's projections. Her assumptions about response rates, sales per average order, and fixed and variable costs may be inaccurate and in need of revision. Start-up year profitability needs to be questioned.

Constraints

Mary currently manages two retail stores, and this appears to occupy much of her time. The addition of a direct mail operation might take too much additional work and possibly jeopardize her successful retail business. As written, there are no budget constraints in this case.

Decision Options

First, Mary could abandon the idea of a catalog and focus her energies on expanding her small chain of retail stores. She should be able to repeat her successful merchandising formula one more time. As mentioned, however, this option entails additional management and transportation headaches. Rethinking her managerial style or selling franchises are further possibilities, but well beyond the scope of advertising management.

Second, Mary could revise her sales forecast upward, and costs downward, and then go ahead with the Neat 'N Tidy catalog. For example, the amount sold per transaction might easily be a little higher than mentioned in the case, while the cost of merchandise might be somewhat lower. Of course, such revisions could be so much wishful thinking.

Third, Mary could devise some other direct mail approach. For example, she might save a great deal of advertising expense by compiling a house list from the names of her retail customers. Although sales would be much lower, she could test her direct marketing mix with relatively little expense.

PREFERRED DECISION

Given the apparent success of so many direct marketing systems, it seems reasonable for Mary to choose to launch a catalog operation. The risks are not particularly high and the long-run growth potential may be substantial. Besides, there is no guarantee that a third retail store will be as successful as the first two. New outlets sometimes fail, even those of successful chains.

More important, extending the sales analysis into the second and third years shows the Neat 'N Tidy catalog becoming increasingly profitable. For example, catalog three will be mailed to a house list of approximately 30,000 (about 20,000 from the second mailing and 10,000 more pulled by the *House*

Beautiful ads). Assuming the same five percent response rate, the same proportionate costs, and somewhat higher overhead, produces a profit of nearly $8,000, calculated as follows:

Sales:	1500 orders	
	× $50 per average order	
	$75,000	

Costs:	$15,000 cost of catalog ($.50 × 30,000)
	37,500 cost of merchandise
	6,655 advertising ($13,309 budget/2)
	8,000 overhead (fees, postage)
	$67,155

Clearly, not all these figures should be taken as completely reliable, but the trend is very encouraging.

QUESTIONS

Guiding Questions

1. How valid are Mary's assumptions? That is, are her estimates of costs, response rates, and average order reasonable? Are they too high or too low? Has she forgotten anything?

2. What happens if Mary extends her sales analysis into the Neat 'N Tidy catalog's second year? Is her goal of making a small profit the first year a reasonable one?

3. Is Mary targeting the right market? Should she focus more directly upon professionals, small businesses, and people with home offices?

Questions for Discussion

1. Direct marketing via catalogs has worked well for many companies. However, is this business as attractive and profitable as it appears? Is it beginning to get overcrowded? Just how frequently do new catalog ventures fail?

2. Can a successful, small retailer also master the rather different business of direct marketing? Designing catalogs and managing a database may require different abilities than displaying merchandise and personally interacting with shoppers.

3. Market research and planning can help to reduce risks, but seldom eliminate them entirely. Should a new business plan, especially one with relatively little downside potential, be more agressively optimistic?

WHAT REALLY HAPPENED

The idea for this case originated in discussions with my wife, who is, at this writing, a full-time mother of two planning her return to paid work. Having been employed by large corporations and having spent many an hour battling southern California traffic, the idea of starting a business that might be operated out of or near our home is an appealing one. Since our investment capital is modest, starting a small catalog firm has been seriously considered.

REFERENCES

American Demographics (1989), "The Big Picture," (March), 22–25.

DMMP: The Direct Marketing MarketPlace (1990), Boca Raton, FL: Hilary House Publishers.

Direct Marketing (1989), "Postage and Paper Hikes Impact 1988 Catalog Activity," (January), 8.

Fisher, Anne B. (1990), "What Consumers Want in the 1990s," *Fortune*, 121 (January 29), 108–112.

Gosden, Freeman, Jr. (1989), "What I Learned From My Mailbox," *Direct Marketing*, (February), 40–47.

Graham, Judith (1989), "DMA Members' Ads Hit $3 Billion," *Advertising Age*, (November 2), 96.

Hawken, Paul (1987), "Mastering the Numbers: How to Develop the Tools You Need for Figuring Out What's Really Happening in Your Business," *Inc.*, (October), 19–20.

Kotler, Philip (1991), *Marketing Management: Analysis, Planning, Implementation, and Control*, 7th ed., Englewood Cliffs, NJ: Prentice-Hall.

Levin, Gary (1991), "Direct Marketers Triumph in Tax Case," *Advertising Age*, (June 24), 12.

Maxwell Sroge Publishing (1989), Denver, Colorado. A division of Maxwell/Sroge Co., Chicago. Telephone contact. 719–633–5556.

Muldoon, Katie (1988), *Catalog Marketing: The Complete Guide to Profitability in the Catalog Business*, 2nd Edition, New York: American Management Association.

Quelch, John A. and Kristina Cannon–Bonventre (1983), "Better Marketing at the Point of Purchase," *Harvard Business Review*, 61 (November – December), 162–169.

Rosenberg, Larry J. and Elizabeth C. Hirschman (1980), "Retailing Without Stores," *Harvard Business Review*, (July – August), 103–112.

Rosser, Jane (1988), "Office in a Box," *Forbes* (March 3), 148–150.

Simross, Lynn (1989), "Got a Problem? No Problem – Just Dial 800-U Name It," *Los Angeles Times* (April 13), Section V, 1, 12.

Simmons Market Research Bureau, Inc. (1988), *1988 Study of Media & Markets*.

SRDS (1991), Wilmette, IL: Standard Rate & Data Service, Inc., February 27.

1989 Statistical Fact Book (1989), Direct Marketing Association, Inc.

Thurmond, Shannon (1988), "Pier 1 Sets Its Course," *Advertising Age* (February 22), 30.

U.S. Industrial Outlook (1991), U.S. Dept. of Commerce, Washington, D.C.

CASE 30

Portage Lake Charter Fishing

TERENCE NEVETT

INTRODUCTION

This case concerns a group of small-budget advertisers whose target audience is difficult to define, who are facing generally unfavorable environmental trends, whose advertising does not seem to be working, and whose resources are severely limited. The case can also be used to introduce a discussion of the practical problems involved in cooperative advertising schemes.

BACKGROUND

Industry

Charter fishing in Michigan is in decline, the number of boats having fallen from 920 in 1985 to 884 by 1989. Apparent reasons include:

- Decline in the quality and quantity of fish.
  (*N.B.* The D.N.R. has increased fish plants to improve stock.)

- Anxiety about contamination
  (There is some disagreement here, with *Outdoor Life* magazine stating that the fish are quite safe to eat.)

There is a change in customer profile. Between 1985 and 1989 the percentage of Michigan customers fell from 70 percent to 62 percent. More out-of-state customers are coming for combined fishing and vacation trips.

Hughes and Blue see themselves as being in the business of family entertainment.

Portage Lake

Onekama has seven boats offering trips from mid-May to mid-October. Their captains charge $250 per half day and $400 for a full day. The advantages of Portage Lake include:

- Excellent location for fishing grounds

- Beautiful approach and setting

- Large, well-equipped boats

- Above-average catch rates

The disadvantages of Portage Lake include:

- Lack of of good class accommodation

- Competition from Ludington

- Remoteness from business and industrial centers

Advertising

Advertising is handled by the captains on an individual basis. Their average expenditure per boat in 1989 was $1850, with the largest item being participation in shows, which rarely pay for themselves directly. There is resistance among the captains to pooling advertising resources. They question how they would share leads, and they want to keep their customer lists for themselves.

PROBLEM STATEMENT

Hughes and Blue believe their advertising is not working because they are failing to communicate effectively with potential customers.

Constraints

Environmental factors

Facilities at Onekama

Limited funds available for advertising

Potential for advertising to contribute (Note Blue's estimate that 80 percent of business are repeats, and of the remainder 80 to 85 percent are referrals.)

Decision Options

The captains could continue to advertise on an individual basis. They could pool their resources in a cooperative campaign. Or they could agree to some form of compromise—perhaps continuing to advertise individually, but using some form of linking theme, device, or logo.

Discussion: When considering these possibilities, students should first focus on what they perceive to be the actual problem. Hughes and Blue may indeed be correct in their view that they are failing to communicate effectively. This may be related to target audience definition, media selection, message, budget size, or a combination. However, the problems posed by unfavorable environmental factors and by the location and character of Onekama are certainly formidable. Are they problems which advertising could reasonably be expected to overcome?

Detailed consideration of advertising costs might consider whether color illustrations on business cards are justifiable, whether attendance at shows is worthwhile, and whether fringe items such as shirts and hats should be eliminated.

PREFERRED OPTION

If the captains can be persuaded to pool their resources, this would give them a combined budget of about $12,000, allowing for individual printing of business cards. They could use generic ads, perhaps based on some theme such as "The Portage Lake Experience"; organize joint mailings; share a booth at the various shows—a considerable saving; share an 800 number for inquiries; and perhaps, lobby jointly for better accommodation at Onekama. There would have to be some compromises, such as allowing captains to keep their individual customer lists, and attention to matters of detail, particularly making certain that rebookings were channeled to the original boat. However, the gains seem to far outweigh the problems of implementation, which are not insuperable.

Simple research could help define the target audience more closely. A questionnaire given to each party could be used to determine whether it was a new or repeat booking, how the respondents heard about Portage Lake, and how they evaluated Portage Lake in comparison with other ports, particularly Ludington.

QUESTIONS
Guiding Questions

How far can the decline in the number of customers and the failure to attract sufficient new ones be attributed to deficiencies in the advertising by Portage captains?

In what ways might the effectiveness of the Portage captains' advertising be improved?

Is a cooperative campaign for the Portage boats likely to be more effective than individual campaigns by each captain?

What problems do the Portage captains face in selecting suitable media?

If Hughes and Blue are correct in their view that they are now in the family entertainment business, what kind of promotional appeals might the Portage captains employ?

Discussion Questions

What kinds of problems confront small advertisers considering a cooperative campaign?

Given the research on the effects of pollution, are there any ethical problems that arise in promoting charter fishing trips on Lake Michigan and encouraging customers to eat their catch?

WHAT ACTUALLY HAPPENED

The captains accepted in principle that some form of cooperation could be beneficial. They agreed to take part in an experimental direct mail campaign and to review the situation when the results became available.

Kleider International Clothing*

Gordon E. Miracle

INTRODUCTION

The purpose of the case is to provide an opportunity for students who are not familiar with international advertising to deal with a few of the international dimensions of the topic. No foreign, international, or cross-cultural experience is assumed. The instructor may want to ask students to obtain further information from secondary sources, playing the role of Ms. Rock who was recently hired with a specific set of responsibilities.

BACKGROUND/OVERVIEW

The case deals with fashion/leisure clothing, a product category familiar to students everywhere. The U.S. and European marketing environments for fashionable leisure attire are mentioned, but not described in detail. Introductory information is given on the Korean market, with some comparisons with the U.S. market. The U.S. and European leisure clothing fashion business is described. It is left to the student to infer whether or not the Asian fashion business may be similar.

PROBLEM STATEMENT

1. Should the company go into Asian markets? If so, in which countries? All at one time, or some first, others later, and if so, in what order?

2. What should be the company's advertising objectives? Advertising message strategies? Advertising media strategies? Advertising budgets? These decisions can be based directly on the standard treatment of these topics in "domestic" cases, taking into consideration the ways in which foreign markets may differ. The instructor can introduce ways in which various country markets are similar or dissimilar. The case is broad, but can be focused according to the instructor's preference, e.g., message objectives and strategies. Because the case is broad, not much depth is expected of the student. The case is intended only to be an introduction to international advertising.

Constraints

With sales of over $250 million, the company has sufficient resources to pursue a range of potentially profitable opportunities.

Decision Options

The alternative courses of action are not indicated at the end of the case. It is up to the student to identify problems and alternative courses of action to solve them. There are large numbers of possible objectives and strategies.

PREFERRED DECISION

None

QUESTIONS

1. What specific steps should Ms. Rock take to carry out her responsibilities?

2. How attractive is each Asian market?

3. How will consumers in each market react to the products offered by Kleider?

4. What competition is likely to be encountered?

5. How should Ms. Rock take into consideration the answers to the above questions 2, 3, 4 to make specific recommendations on advertising objectives and strategies?

6. Should a *lead advertising agency* be used to prepare centrally the advertising objectives and strategies to be used in foreign markets? Will local advertising agencies be required?

TEACHING TIPS

The instructor should give students considerable guidance before they prepare the case for classroom discussion. Even the points that are simple and obvious to an experienced international advertising professional will not be obvious to most students.

Students find the subjects of fashion leisure clothing and international advertising relevant and interesting. They are able to relate to the important issue of standardization versus localization. They understand the need to pay attention to cultural differences when making decisions on advertising objectives, strategies, and executions. However, students without international experience necessarily respond to cultural issues based on gut feel and guesses. Often they perceive that Asian cultures are likely to be sensitive to portrayals of physical contact, as displayed in the Streetlife campaign, and they guess that Asians may not be as accepting of this theme as Europeans. However, they are unable to suggest reasonable alternatives with confidence, which allows the instructor to point out the need for "local" input or evaluation of centralized policies.

CASE 32

Texas Tapes Audio Stores*

John M. Schleede

INTRODUCTION

The purpose of this case is to give the student an opportunity to develop a simple media schedule around defined parameters. In the case, Fred Hardy, the marketing manager for Texas Tapes, is trying to decide how much of his limited budget should be placed in newspapers and how much in radio. In both cases, the decision of which radio stations or newspapers is an important factor. Finally, the student should be able to recommend a specific month-by-month schedule.

OVERVIEW

Consumer Behavior: Fred probably assumes that the consumer knows what music he or she wants to purchase, so the question from his perspective is how to get them to buy it at Texas Tapes. This is probably a low involvement decision for many consumers. Therefore, they are aware of the alternative choices for purchasing music: mass merchandiser, specialty store, etc. If this is the case, then Fred's assumption about the nature of his advertising objective is correct. First, Texas Tapes must build and maintain share of mind, and second, they must draw consumers into the store.

With regard to which consumers to target, there are two distinct segments given: rock listeners and country music lovers. Since these segments have different characteristics and differing media habits, Texas Tapes must reach both segments with their advertising media. In the absence of any additional information, the student should probably weight both groups relatively equally in media exposure. Students are often tempted to spend more money on the rock segment, which should be discouraged unless they can demonstrate that rock has more potential.

Competition: Nothing is said in the case about Texas Tapes' direct competition except to point out that it is an extremely competitive environment. Besides being the third of all the music outlets in market share, Texas Tapes must deal with the discounting practices of mass merchandisers who sell their products relatively cheaply and place considerable pressure on small retailers like Fred.

Other Considerations:

1. With a limited budget, cost efficiency is an important factor in selecting media vehicles.

2. Forty percent of all the business is conducted in the last quarter of the year.

PROBLEM STATEMENT

The problem is to develop a media schedule which incorporates all of the decisions Fred Hardy must make in his analysis.

Decision Options

1. Newspapers vs. Radio

One decision is the relative amount of media weight to be allocated between the two media classes. Students often question the necessity of using newspapers, especially given the efficient nature of radio. However, students should be reminded that there are two goals for the advertising: maintaining share of mind and getting customers into the stores. Although radio can accomplish the first, it will not be as effective at announcing the sales. Students might argue that rock listeners don't read newspapers, but they should be reminded that country listeners do (and so do rock listeners, although to a lesser extent).

How much money to allocate to newspapers should be determined by the advertising objective. Ideally, an advertisement per week would help to maintain share of mind while keeping customers coming through the door. However, limited resources will prevent that from occurring. Assuming that Fred would want to use both newspapers, for about $100,000 he can advertise once per month for 8 months and twice per month for the last four months of the year. This would give approximately twice the weight during the quarter when most of the business is done and include the month leading up to the busy period.

Some students will argue that only the *Houston Chronicle* should be used because of its larger circulation. However, it is likely that while there is some overlap, most of the readership comes from different segments. In totaling the two ratings for the newspapers, still only 66 percent of all adults are covered.

2. *Radio: 60s vs. 30s, Fixed vs. ROS*

The choice of length of the radio commercials should be determined by the job to be accomplished. If learning is the goal, the emphasis should be on 60s. However if awareness is the goal, the additional commercials gained by using 30s will make them the preferred option. In this case, since the newspapers will be announcing the sales, 30s should be sufficient to build and maintain share of mind.

The use of fixed position commercials allows the advertiser to pinpoint when his commercials will air. In addition, the number of persons reached by each spot will be higher. ROS spots will reach fewer persons per spot, but have the potential to reach more persons in total as the cume audiences will be higher. Some students will argue for using a blend of the two, and there is nothing wrong with that approach. An analysis of CPM will be useful in making this decision. To evaluate CPM, the students should use the following formula:

$$CPM = \frac{Spot\ Cost \times 1000}{Avg.\ Persons}$$

For KIKK-FM the respective CPM's are:

$$ROS\ 30 \quad \$7.54 = \frac{\$175 \times 1000}{23,300}$$

$$Fixed\ 30 \quad \$9.37 = \frac{\$325 \times 1000}{34,700}$$

In general, the ROS spots are the most cost efficient.

3. *Which Radio Stations?*

The process of vehicle analysis should call for a weighted decision based on audience size, cost efficiency, and format. In the absence of information to the contrary, the radio dollars should be split between country and rock formats.

PREFERRED DECISIONS

You will get as many solutions as there are students. Included is one possible solution which reaches about 90 percent of the target audience about three times per month during the crucial last four months of the year. A maintenance schedule of 75 percent reach with a frequency of about two for the rest of the year is included.

Texas Tapes Media Schedule For Fiscal Year 1991

Target Audience: Adults 25–34

Target Audience Size: 1,163,200

Media Budget: $155,864 (99.0%)

Contingency: $1,574 (1.0%)

Number of Insertions per Month

Media Vehicles	Yearly Ads	Yearly Cost (000)	JAN	FEB	MAR	APR	MAY	JUN
Local Newspapers	32	$97.5	2	2	2	2	2	2
Chronicle	16	$50.5	1	1	1	1	1	1
Post	16	$47.0	1	1	1	1	1	1
Spot Radio	588	$58.4	37	37	37	37	37	37
KKBQ-FM	76	$6.8	5	5	5	5	5	5
KLOL	320	$35.2	20	20	20	20	20	20
KRBE-FM	192	$16.3	12	12	12	12	12	12
Total		$155.9						
Local Newspapers		($000)	$6	$6	$6	$6	$6	$6
Spot Radio		($000)	$4	$4	$4	$4	$4	$4
Monthly Totals		($000)	$10	$10	$10	$10	$10	$10
Effective Reach			84.8%	84.8%	84.8%	84.8%	84.8%	84.8%
Gross Rating Points			172.9	172.9	172.9	172.9	172.9	172.9
CPM Impressions			$4.88	$4.88	$4.88	$4.88	$4.88	$4.88

Texas Tapes Media Schedule For Fiscal Year 1991

Target Audience: Adults 25–34

Target Audience Size: 1,163,200

Media Budget: $155,864 (99.0%)

Contingency: $1,574 (1.0%)

Number of Insertions per Month

Media Vehicles	Yearly Ads	Yearly Cost (000)	JUL	AUG	SEP	OCT	NOV	DEC
Local Newspapers	32	$97.5	2	2	4	4	4	4
Chronicle	16	$50.5	1	1	2	2	2	2
Post	16	$47.0	1	1	2	2	2	2
Spot Radio	588	$58.4	37	37	73	73	73	73
KKBQ-FM	76	$6.8	5	5	9	9	9	9
KLOL	320	$35.2	20	20	40	40	40	40
KRBE-FM	192	$16.3	12	12	24	24	24	24
Total		$155.9						
Local Newspapers		($000)	$6	$6	$12	$12	$12	$12
Spot Radio		($000)	$4	$4	$7	$7	$7	$7
Monthly Totals		($000)	$10	$10	$19	$19	$19	$19
Effective Reach			84.8%	84.8%	96.2%	96.2%	96.2%	96.2%
Gross Rating Points			172.9	172.9	342.2	342.2	342.2	342.2
CPM Impressions			$4.88	$4.88	$4.88	$4.88	$4.88	$4.88

CASE 33

A&A Electric Limited of India*

KARTIK PASHUPATI

INTRODUCTION

This case deals with a situation where a largely unadvertised product (electrical switches for home use) is seeking to establish a brand identity and preference through marketing communication, including advertising. In the process, it raises interesting issues in several areas of advertising management: the need for advertising in the marketing communications mix for such a product, the presence of budget constraints, the appropriateness of the creative strategy, the appropriateness of the proposed media strategy, and the problems involved in cross-cultural communication, even among joint-venture collaborators.

BACKGROUND/OVERVIEW

The critical internal and external factors in the case can be analyzed using the framework of strengths, weaknesses, opportunities, and threats.

Internal Factors (Strengths and Weaknesses)

Strengths:

A superior product, backed up by a collaboration with WK Electric Ltd.

The instinctive appeal in the Indian market of a "foreign" collaboration

Multifusion Advertising's track record of producing successful creative campaigns

The A&A Group's extensive manufacturing experience in the electrical sector

A&A's apparent willingness to use both formal and informal market research

Weaknesses:
The A&A Group's lack of experience in consumer marketing and Mr. Swamy's lack of experience in consumer markets

The relatively low advertising budget

A&A's lack of an extensive distribution network

The relatively higher price of Powerlux – WK accessories

External Factors (Opportunities and Threats)

Opportunities:
A rapidly growing market (12 percent per annum over the last five years), fueled by the construction boom

The government's liberalized industrial policy, enabling new entrants into the market

The receptivity of specifiers to premium brands of accessories, such as CEL and Sputnik

The receptivity of home owners to decor-oriented electrical accessories, such as CEL and Sputnik

The near-total absence of competitive advertising means that
achieving significant share-of-voice for a new entrant is not much of a problem

Threats:
Existing competition, especially from Sailboat (which has a well-established brand name and the ability to deal shrewdly with environmental constraints, such as government regulation)

Competition from new entrants such as Avanti – Wilhelm and Sailboat's "Silk-line" series

A new nationwide advertising campaign from Avanti – Wilhelm

Consumers' low involvement with the product category

Consumers' lack of genuine concern about the safety (or danger) of existing electrical accessories

Other Critical Factors

The existence of multiple target audiences: consumers, specifiers, traders

The limited availability of specialized media targeted at specifiers, and the absence of regional editions of national magazines

The limited literacy of electricians makes it difficult to reach them through print media

PROBLEM STATEMENT

How should Mr. Shah and Mr. Swamy respond to Multifusion's campaign proposal?

Constraints

The weaknesses and threats cited in *Other Critical Factors* above provide a good indication of some of the constraints to be considered while analyzing the case. Specifically, attention can be drawn to the likelihood of increased competition following the change in the regulatory environment, and A&A Electric's limited advertising budget, coupled with the non-availability of regional editions of national magazines targeted toward specifiers.

Decision Options

Some of the alternatives open to the management of A&A Electric are as follows:

1. Adopt Multifusion's creative strategy and media strategy without question, and try to explain to Holbrook that local market conditions demand deviations from international norms.
   Possible drawbacks: This alternative might result in a higher budget than necessary and some wasted exposure in areas where A&A is not yet ready to launch Powerlux – WK accessories.

2. Adopt Multifusion's creative strategy, but restrict media usage to newspapers alone, for launch and co-op advertising. Non-media efforts could proceed as before.
   Possible drawbacks: This alternative would result in a reduced frequency of exposure to architects and designers, and could also give the benefit of a greater share of voice to Avanti – Wilhelm and other new entrants to the market. It would deprive Powerlux – WK accessories of any pioneer advantages they might otherwise be able to claim.

3. Do not adopt Multifusion's recommendations on either creative or media strategy, but ask them to re-work both in order to target specifiers and dealers only.
   Possible drawbacks: Creative strategy is not really a major bone of contention, even for Holbrook; such a proposal will only alienate the agency and make it reconsider its decision to accept the A&A Electric account. The agency (Rodriguez) has also clearly put some thought into its media recommendations; hence, rejecting them off-hand without serious thought may not serve any purpose.

PREFERRED DECISION

A&A Electric should accept Multifusion's recommendations regarding creative and media strategy. The wasted exposure on a national level might be well worth the marginal extra expense, in order to stimulate trade interest in Powerlux – WK accessories even beyond the launch region and to pre-empt Avanti – Wilhelm as the pioneer in new-technology electrical accessories in the Indian market.

An alternative to magazines could be to use direct mail, with a fairly high frequency, as a means of reaching architects and other specifiers. This would get over the problem of wasted exposure stated by Holbrook. However, printing and postage costs associated with direct mail might well turn out to be higher than the extra cost of national magazines; hence suggesting this alternative (with its attendant costs) might help overcome Holbrook's objections without ruffling his ego.

QUESTIONS
Guiding Questions

What is the role of advertising in the marketing communications mix for a product such as domestic electrical accessories?

Given the findings of A&A's market research, are Multifusion's recommendations regarding *creative strategy* appropriate for Powerlux – WK accessories?

Should A&A accept Multifusion's rationale for its *media recommendations?*

Should A&A proceed with a national advertising campaign despite the fact that its initial launch will be purely regional?

Does David Holbrook have a point, or is he being insensitive to the realities of the local marketplace?

Discussion Questions

Is consumer advertising appropriate for a product such as electrical wiring accessories? Under what circumstances would such advertising be appropriate?

In the light of the market research findings presented in the case, discuss Multifusion's creative strategy recommendations. Do you think it might be a better idea to try and educate consumers about the importance of safety in electrical accessories, instead of trying to position Powerlux – WK as "decorator switches?"

Given the circumstances presented in the case, do you agree with Multifusion's media recommendations?

Advise Mr. Shah and Mr. Swamy what response they should give to Multifusion Advertising.

WHAT ACTUALLY HAPPENED

This case is a condensed version of a factual situation, and the names of companies and individuals, as well as the order of some events have been changed. In the actual situation, "A&A Electric" accepted the advertising agency's recommendations and was able to establish a parity position with "Avanti – Wilhelm" in the national market. The national roll-out was delayed slightly due to production problems, and A&A withdrew from the national media at this time to conserve funds. However, once the roll-out resumed, A&A's competitive pricing, combined with its superior salesperson network, enabled it to establish a satisfactory presence in the larger urban markets and achieve a better market share than Avanti – Wilhelm in the premium segment of the electrical accessories market. "Sailboat" remains the unquestioned market leader in the overall accessories market.

Walpurgis Films—Home Videos*

TERENCE NEVETT

INTRODUCTION

This case is based around an actual promotion that involved the use of live snakes. It confronts students with two issues: first, the perennial one of the original idea that could have considerable impact but may not be feasible; and second, the situation that arises when a manager has misgivings about a course of action favored by a superior but lacks the authority to prevent it.

BACKGROUND

The home video market is estimated to be worth some $10 billion. Walpurgis is an independent production company targeting the sci-fi, fantasy, and horror segment. It believes its audience is loyal and growing. Walpurgis advertises aggressively to consumers and retailers. Its consumer advertising includes MTV and Fox, and print ads in specialist media, as well as comic book versions of its films. It targets retailers with direct mail, advertising in trade publications, and a variety of promotional support items.

Walpurgis is soon to release *Snake Woman*, which President and C.E.O. Ray Sved believes can be a big success. Sved want to use live snakes for POP display, in spite of the reservations of his director of marketing, Rick Perez.

PROBLEM STATEMENT

There are really two levels of problem to consider:

- The specific problem: is Sved's idea for the snake promotion feasible and in the best interests of Walpurgis Films?

- The general problem: how should a member of an organization react when confronted with a superior pushing an idea that seems to have unfortunate implications?

Constraints

- Sved's enthusiasm for the snake promotion; will not easily be deflected

- The relative positions of Sved and Perez in the organization

- The need for a high-impact promotion

- The cost of the promotion (Walpurgis cannot afford to supply all its retailers.)

- Practical difficulties involved in the promotion: distributing the snakes, arranging for them to be fed, arrangements for the snakes after the promotion

- The character of the market Walpurgis is serving

Decision Options

If Walpurgis Films goes ahead with the snake promotion, they are taking a calculated risk. Sved seems to be setting out deliberately to provoke controversy, as evidenced by his proposal to send snakes to video critics. Given the type of production in which the company specializes and the segment it targets, the risks involved would be less that for a more "orthodox" production company. In fact, Walpurgis' customers might be quite pleased at upsetting some of the more staid video store customers. However, the store owners might be more of a problem since they would not wish to antagonize their clientele. Walpurgis would also have to resolve questions related to the care and feeding of snakes in the stores, as well as the problem of what is to happen to them at the end of the promotion.

A further difficulty is the position of the dealers who do not receive snakes. Either they will receive no support, in which case Walpurgis will have to rely on spin-off from the major promotion; or they will have special material created for them, in which case the total promotional package for *Snake Woman* becomes too expensive. (One of Sved's arguments in favor of the snake idea is that it would save money.) The promotion would almost certainly provoke an outcry from animal rights activists. Walpurgis seems likely to be accused of degrading snakes and leaving them open to abuse and ill-treatment by dealers and customers. The fate of the snakes at the end of the promotion is also likely to come under close scrutiny.

Perez is in a difficult position personally. He can see the problems involved in the promotion, but his C.E.O. is not prepared to consider any argument. The political reality in many organizations would be that if Perez becomes fully involved in the promotion and it fails, then he would be held responsible. On the other hand, if he voices his opposition and the promotion fails, he will still be blamed because the cause will be identified as his lack of enthusiasm.

PREFERRED OPTION

The snake idea has superficial appeal and would probably represent a high-impact promotion for a limited number of dealers. However, it is fraught with practical problems to the extent that it is probably not feasible. There is also no satisfactory alternative for the large number of dealers who would not be able to receive snakes. In addition, there are considerable indirect costs involved in negotiating for the snakes, arranging for their distribution (which seems likely to be very complicated), negotiating what is to happen to them after the promotion, and so on. Perez therefore runs the risk of associating himself with a fiasco. His best course, since Sved seems not to listen to counterarguments in meetings, is probably to put something in writing, perhaps a brief report setting out the case against the snake idea in careful detail. If Sved still goes ahead, Perez must give the promotion his full support to avoid any suspicion that he is sabotaging it. At the same time, he might begin looking for another job!

QUESTIONS
Guiding Questions

Is the snake promotion feasible? Would it have the kind of impact that Sved believes?

Could Walpurgis achieve similar impact without the use of live snakes—for example, by using realistic moving models?

What action should Perez take if he believes the campaign will be unsuccessful?

Is Sved correct in saying "Any sort of publicity is good publicity" (a) for Walpurgis or (b) for business organizations generally?

Discussion Questions

Does the use of live animals and reptiles raise any ethical problems for the advertising manager?

Is a manager's first duty to an organization to obey the instructions of a superior, even if that superior is believed to be wrong?

WHAT ACTUALLY HAPPENED

The company went ahead with the promotion without having resolved the feeding problem. Animal protection officials, who received many calls from unhappy dealers, publicly condemned the whole idea as cruel and inhuman, and called on the company to take the snakes back. Media were told the snakes were in danger because they were not being properly fed. The response from dealers was unfavorable.

TEACHING SUGGESTIONS

This is a case to which students are able to relate on a personal level, which tends to make for lively discussion. It offers plenty of opportunity for role play: Perez and Sved, Sved or Perez and a complaining dealer, a Walpurgis dealer and a shocked elderly customer, etc.